Lucan Lives

Lucan Lives

Chief Inspector
DAVID GERRING

as told to
ROBERT BRIMMELL

ROBERT HALE · LONDON

© David Gerring & Robert Brimmell 1995
First published in Great Britain 1995

ISBN 0 7090 5559 5

Robert Hale Limited
Clerkenwell House
Clerkenwell Green
London EC1R 0HT

The right of David Gerring & Robert Brimmell to be identified as
authors of this work has been asserted by them
in accordance with the Copyright, Designs and
Patents Act 1988.

2 4 6 8 10 9 7 5 3 1

Photoset in Ehrhardt by
Derek Doyle & Associates, Mold, Clwyd.
Printed in Great Britain by
St Edmundsbury Press Ltd, Bury St Edmunds, Suffolk.
Bound by WBC Book Manufacturers Limited,
Bridgend, Mid-Glamorgan.

Contents

List of Illustrations   7
Foreword   9
Prologue   11

1	Body in a Bag	17
2	The House of Horror	22
3	Bad Day at Balaclava	31
4	The Warrior Breed	38
5	Family at War	46
6	The Hand that Rocked The Cradle	54
7	The Upstairs, Downstairs Murder	62
8	Last Throw of the Dice	70
9	The Perfect Murder	79
10	Man on the Run	88
11	The Eton Mafia	97
12	Spinning Drums	105
13	Five Just Men	115
14	The Nob Squad	123
15	Caught in the Spider's Web	131
16	The Gorilla Man	140
17	The Inquest Verdict	147
18	Chasing False Trails	158
19	The Goldenballs Case	166
20	Last Refuge of a Scoundrel	172
21	The Trial of Lord Lucan	180

Index   189

Illustrations

between pages 64 and 65

1. Examining some of the evidence with Roy Ranson
2. Lord Lucan's mother, the Dowager Countess, and his brother-in-law William Shand Kydd
3. Lord Lucan and his bride Veronica after their wedding in November 1963
4. The first of many newspaper headlines which appeared on the day after Sandra Rivett's death
5. Hotel proprietress Suzanne Guilpain with Roy Ranson, me and interpreter Glynne Rhys-Evans
6. Susan Maxwell-Scott and her husband Ian
7. Sandra Rivett, the nanny brutally beaten to death at 46 Lower Belgrave Street
8. Talking to a diver probing the harbour at Newhaven for Lord Lucan's body
9. With the press corps at a seafront bar in St Malo
10. With then Prime Minister Harold Wilson and my wife Pat, and Roy and Irene Ranson
11. A cartoon by Wren which appeared on my retirement from the Metropolitan Police
12. John Aspinall after being punched for what he said at the memorial service for Lord Lucan's friend Dominic Elwes

PICTURE CREDITS

Mirror Syndication International: 1, 2, 3, 12. *Evening Standard*/Solo: 4. Daily Express Syndication Department: 5. Topham: 6. London News Service: 7. *Evening Argus* Brighton: 8. Geoffrey White: 9. Joe Bulaitis/Camera Press: 10. *Western Mail* Cardiff: 11.

Foreword

Let me straightaway declare a personal interest in the Lucan story. In 1974 I had already spent twelve years producing and presenting the very first regular TV programme dedicated to inviting viewers to 'help the police with their enquiries'. Unlike the programmes that followed in its path, *Police Five* was essentially a 'police programme' – the crimes were chosen by them and they had editorial control over what was said and what was shown on screen. My task was simply to discuss what was needed and to shape it into interesting and successful television. The weekly access to a wide spread of potential witnesses, fifty weeks of the year, was invaluable, and *Police Five* became as much a part of criminal investigation as the forensic, fingerprint, and photographic departments. The squad investigating the murder of the Lucan family nanny used it on several occasions. In the early stages it was to find anyone who might have been near the scene of the crime on that fateful night. Later it was used to revive flagging public interest in the search for Lord Lucan as trail after trail went cold.

Dave Gerring's account of the murder and the subsequent hue and cry makes fascinating reading. It is, as one would expect of a senior police officer and experienced investigator, essentially factual, clear-headed and without dramatics, leaving the reader to draw his or her own conclusions on how a named and famed murderer could virtually 'disappear from the face of the earth'. The sting is in the tail! Only at the very end does Dave Gerring indulge in supposition, and an intriguing supposition it is. Hours later, as I am given the pleasure of penning this foreword, I am still pondering on it!

Shaw Taylor

Prologue

The evening of Thursday 7 November 1974 was wet and cold, a trough of low pressure bringing with it sheets of drizzle on a southerly wind which swirled through London's West End. Collars turned up, theatregoers scurried to see *Sleuth* at the Fortune, while Agatha Christie's whodunit, *The Mousetrap*, was in its twenty-second year at the St Martin's. Somewhat less propitiously for the forces of law and order, *Jack the Ripper* was being staged at the Ambassadors, a musical based on the prostitute killer who stalked the East End in the 1880s, thought by some to be an aristocrat, and never caught. The lights of the neon-lit cinemas were reflected on the wet pavement in Leicester Square while, well away from Piccadilly Circus and Soho, the dark canyons of sullen streets were largely deserted, most people content to stay indoors and watch the night's offerings on TV. *The Six Million Dollar Man*, *This Week* and a *Father Brown* detective story entitled 'The Dagger With Wings' featured on Thames; *Mastermind* and a play by David Edgar, *Baby Love*, on BBC1; *Monty Python* and *The Complete Victor Borge* on BBC2. As they watched their screens a 10 lb bomb exploded without warning in the crowded King's Arms public house opposite the Royal Artillery Barracks at Woolwich, killing one and injuring twenty-eight, latest of a succession of IRA terrorist attacks on the capital.

In the Plumbers Arms, several miles away in more fashionable SW1 at 14 Lower Belgrave Street close to Victoria Station and a short walk from Buckingham Palace, there was much else for regulars to talk about in the warmth of the lounge bar. The day before, Leeds had beaten Hungarian league leaders Ujpest Dozsa in the second round, second leg, of the European Cup and Derby had seen off Athlético Madrid in the UEFA Cup. In the first game of their Rugby Union tour the awesome All

Blacks had unexpectedly struggled to beat a Combined Universities squad 10–3.

Those not interested in sport chatted about news and politics. In America Gerald Ford had replaced Richard Nixon, who had resigned over the Watergate scandal. A crucial ruling was awaited from Judge Sirica at the cover-up trial on whether or not the White House tapes would be declared admissible. There was widespread media speculation that Ted Heath's days were numbered as Leader of the Conservative Party after losing the General Election the previous month to Harold Wilson and a Labour government with a majority of just three. Inflation was galloping along, the cost of living set to rise twenty per cent on the year in the face of crippling wage demands and the soaring cost of raw materials.

At 9.50 p.m. conversation ground to an abrupt halt, a dozen pairs of eyes swivelling in unison to the door as it burst open with a clatter and a petite woman staggered in, damp and bedraggled. She was barefooted, wearing a brown polo neck jumper over a green pinafore dress heavily soaked with blood which poured from a number of deep cuts on the right side of her head, matting her fair hair and running down her rain-streaked face in scarlet rivulets.

The pub, one of two in the street, was on the fringe of Belgravia and not much frequented by those well-heeled residents who lived lives closeted by wealth in expensively bought privacy. But head barman Derrick Whitehouse recognized the distraught woman as one of the nearby residents in Lower Belgrave Street who did occasionally call in to the pub to buy cigarettes. She was clearly in a blind panic, badly hurt and frightened for her life.

'Help me, help me,' she stammered hysterically. 'I've just escaped from a murderer ... he's in the house ... he's murdered the nanny.'

The startled barman reacted quickly, coming from behind his bar and leading the terrified woman to a bench seat where he gently laid her down on her back. He tried to calm and comfort her, drawing on experience gained while working at Great Ormond Street Children's Hospital. His wife brought towels to staunch the blood coursing from seven ugly wounds to her scalp and on her forehead. The unfortunate woman had obviously been the victim of a savage attack.

Prologue

'My children ... my children,' she kept repeating deliriously. 'I'm dying. I think my neck has been broken. He tried to strangle me.'

The barman placed a blanket over her and made a 999 call to summon an ambulance and the police. The call went to New Scotland Yard and was telexed through to Gerald Road Police Station half-a-mile away from Lower Belgrave Street. It said: *Person assaulted. Ambulance called. Distressed female.*

The London Ambulance Service logged their call at 9.57 p.m. and an ambulance was directed to Lower Belgrave Street from the headquarters in Waterloo Road, its flashing light illuminating the terrace of elegant houses running up to Eaton Square. Trainee supervisor Frederick Strahan and ambulanceman Martin Broom put a dressing on the woman's wounds before taking her in the ambulance to the casualty department at St George's Hospital at Hyde Park Corner. PC Stanley Chapman had already been at the Plumbers Arms when the ambulance arrived and he went with them to the hospital where the woman underwent emergency treatment and was admitted to a private room.

At the time none of the incredulous drinkers in the bar realized they had witnessed the opening scene of a drama that was to become one of the world's most baffling murder mysteries. The injured woman was Lady Veronica Lucan, estranged wife of a man whose name was destined to enter the annals of crime history: Lord Lucan.

One customer, Cevald Olavsen, a courier at the Norwegian Embassy, had been able to find out from the woman her address. He left the pub and went up the street to No. 46 where he found the front door shut. There was a light in an upstairs window but the lower part of the house was in darkness. He decided to wait at the house for the police.

When uniformed Police Sergeant Donald Baker and Police Constable Christopher Baddick arrived, they forced the door to make their way into the darkened house. In upstairs bedrooms were the Lucan's three young children – Frances, ten, George, seven, and Camilla, four.

It was in the basement breakfast room they made the horrific discovery that was to spark off an amazing murder mystery. The body of the children's nanny, Sandra Rivett, was stuffed in a canvas United States mail-bag for evident disposal. She had gone down to make tea and had been bludgeoned to death by an assailant waiting in the darkness.

Lady Veronica had also been attacked when she went looking for the nanny. As she called out the nanny's name in the darkness on the landing at the entrance door to the basement, a man rushed out of a cloakroom and struck her several heavy blows on the head. When she fell to the ground bleeding and screaming, gloved fingers were stuck into her mouth and she was told to 'shut up' by a voice she recognized as her husband's. She bit his fingers and, as he put his hands round her neck in an attempt to strangle her, she struggled and managed to subdue him by grabbing and twisting his testicles. They sat exhausted on the stairs and she talked for her life, eventually calming him down and persuading him to take her to her bedroom. While he went into the bathroom to soak towels to bathe her wounds, she escaped when she heard the taps running and dashed 100 metres through the rain to find sanctuary at the Plumbers Arms.

It was, seemingly, a case of mistaken identity – a meticulously planned murder that went tragically awry in the darkness of the basement kitchen because the nanny had changed her night off. The murder weapon, a blood-stained length of lead pipe wrapped in adhesive tape, was found near the basement doorway.

Of the debonair aristocrat Lord Lucan there was no sign. He fled from the house and vanished that night into thin air, never to be found by the authorities despite a worldwide manhunt and numerous reported sightings. The sporting peer, known to his friends as 'Lucky' for his skills at the gaming tables, was named by a coroner's jury as the murderer of not-so-lucky Nanny Rivett. He was the last man in Britain to be branded a murderer by a coroner's jury and was committed in his absence for trial to the Old Bailey. A warrant for his arrest remains gathering dust in Scotland Yard files, waiting to be served.

Is Lord Lucan still alive or did he take the gentleman's way out and commit suicide following that fateful night when he discovered, to his horror, that he had killed the wrong woman? Did loyal friends spirit him out of the country? Is he now living in hiding with a new identity, his face perhaps altered through plastic surgery? Did he even commit the brutal murder at all, or was it the work of a contract killer he hired? These are questions which have bewildered and intrigued criminologists for two decades, questions which remain unanswered.

The story of the events immediately following the brutal murder of Sandra Rivett are well chronicled and familiar. Much has been written since then about the killing and the unsuccessful search for the 7th Earl of Lucan, some of it totally inaccurate and wildly fanciful. Fact has merged with fiction and Lord Lucan had become almost a legendary figure from a lost age, like Robin Hood and Davy Crockett.

As a top detective directly involved in the incredible murder investigation and abortive hunt, I believe I know what may have really happened to the elusive Lord Lucan. I interviewed key players in what became known as the Lucan Set to unravel their dark secrets. It was my task to try and break down the impregnable wall of silence erected by privileged people who believed their wealth and outdated code of honour among friends set them above the law.

This is the true story of the Lucan Affair, authoritatively told from an insider's point of view in a Murder Squad whose officers were accused of a cover-up and were ridiculed for being out of their social depth among the aristocracy, that most impenetrable of British institutions. The narrative is both tragic and hilariously funny, capturing the spirit of the early 1970s when the Swinging Sixties dissolved amid miners' strikes and the three-day working week.

1 Body in a Bag

Many people remember exactly what they were doing when they first heard President Kennedy was assassinated. In much the same way I remember how I first got involved in the hunt for Lord Lucan, a frustrating search that was to take over the majority of my working life for a year and absorb my thinking to this day. At the time it seemed no more than a routine murder inquiry that would soon be sorted out, different only in that it had taken place at the home of an earl and therefore had to be conducted with the sensitivity we tactfully accorded the good and the great.

I was at home with my family at Orpington in the South East London commuter belt, having clocked off from Gerald Road Police Station at 6 p.m. after a routine working day. It was a ten-minute walk to Victoria Station. At Victoria I dropped in for a beer at the Shakespeare pub while waiting to catch the 7.12 train. My wife, Pat, picked me up at the station and, once home, I had dinner and spent the evening reading and watching TV like everyone else. I was about to go to bed shortly after 11 p.m. when the phone rang. I picked it up, hoping it wasn't going to be the office and another lost night of sleep.

'Guvnor, we've got a nasty murder,' said a voice I immediately recognized as Detective Sergeant Graham Forsyth, who was on late turn that night.

'What's the score?' I asked.

'We've got a body at Lower Belgrave Street, a woman. We think she's a children's nanny. She's in a big bag in the basement.'

'Who is she?'

'We think her name is Sandra Rivett. She's the nanny for Lady Lucan. Lady Lucan's been assaulted, too. She's been taken to St George's Hospital with head injuries.'

'Is she likely to die?'

'No, she's badly hurt but expected to live.'

'What about Lord Lucan?'

'Apparently they're separated. We can't find him. We're looking for him now. He has a mews house in Eaton Row, just round the back of Lower Belgrave Street. I've checked that with DC Stewart and he isn't there. He's got another flat in Elizabeth Street. I'm going round there to have a look at that.'

'What about children?'

'Yes, there's three of them. They're all right. They've been taken off by Lucan's mother to her home at St John's Wood. A PC has gone with them to keep an eye on them.'

My mind was racing ahead. I didn't know Lord Lucan but I knew he lived on our manor along with a lot of other prominent people who inhabited Belgravia. Many of the properties were owned by the Duke of Westminster and Lord Cadogan and, while a lot of nouveau riche property developers and oil-rich Arabs had moved in, there was still a sprinkling of titled residents. I was one of the few Metropolitan Police officers who kept in my office copies of *Who's Who*, *Debrett's* and *Burke's Peerage* – the top people's 'stud books'. It was an unwritten rule a senior officer from Gerald Road would attend at the scene of any sudden death, whether foul play or suicide. Not surprisingly, the name Lord Lucan immediately set alarm bells ringing.

'OK, I'll be right up,' I said. 'Get one of our own people on the door at the house, make sure they get everyone else out. Don't allow anybody in until I get there. Get somebody to guard Lady Lucan at the hospital and set up a murder squad office.'

Sergeant Forsyth was an experienced officer, and I knew he would get the ball rolling by the time I reached Gerald Road. When he rang off I called my boss, Detective Superintendent Roy Ranson, who lived at Bromley, and gave him a brief résumé of what had happened and the action that was already being taken.

I drove to Gerald Road and got there at 1 a.m., and Roy Ranson arrived a little later. By then the police station was buzzing. A room had been found on the first floor and had been cleared in preparation for use as the murder squad office.

Gerald Road was a pleasant police station, neat and clean with flowers outside in summer in window boxes and tubs on the pavement. Officers would climb up a step ladder to lovingly water baskets of geraniums hanging from the bracket supporting the traditional blue lamp above the front door. If Jack Warner had walked out and said 'Evening All' it wouldn't have come as a surprise. Noel Coward once lived in the narrow road of white-fronted houses, but the police station was squeezed between the luxury homes and its days were numbered.

By the 1970s the great days of Belgravia were largely over, with many of the once grand houses split into flats after the war or used as foreign embassies. But some aristocrats stayed on or retained a *pied-à-terre*, often in mews which had once been stables and housed impoverished coachmen and servants employed by their families in earlier times. They still retained an attitude to the police I hadn't come across at previous stations I had been at in the West End and South London. When they rang up they would automatically expect to speak to a senior officer – the engineer, not the oily rag, as they would put it. Constables making house calls would sometimes promote themselves to sergeant in order to make themselves acceptable to the inheritors of the world whose lives were dictated by the seasons: Klosters and Gstaad in spring; Cap d'Antibes, Marbella and the Greek Islands in summer; the Caribbean in winter.

By the time I arrived the major incident cupboard had already been broken open to kit out the office. Everything was kept in the sealed cupboard – books, pencils, rubbers, message pads, even rubber bands – so an operational office could instantly be up and running. The GPO would soon be there to put in dedicated telephone lines.

I sat down with Roy Ranson in my office and updated him on what had been happening. Basically what we had was a body in a basement we thought belonged to the nanny, Sandra Rivett. Lady Veronica Lucan was in hospital, injured and under guard; the Lucan children had been taken to a place of safety with their widowed grandmother and Lord Lucan himself was being sought. That wasn't bad for starters. The case already had the makings of a winner: dead servant, missing master.

Roy had a sharp brain and a keen eye for detail. He was less outgoing than I was and people said that together we made a good team. We worked closely on many cases and I don't think we ever had any disagreements on what needed to be done. Roy Ranson had once been with the Flying Squad but the highlight of his career had come earlier in the year, on 20 March, when Princess Anne had been attacked. A gunman ambushed her car in the Mall, intent on kidnapping her and demanding a £1 million ransom. Ian Ball fired six shots, injuring her chauffeur, a police bodyguard and a passenger from a taxi who intervened, before he fled into St James's Park and was arrested. The incident was soon sorted out with Ball under lock and key, but the ramifications rumbled on, begging questions over the protection of the Royals. A bullet had gone between Princess Anne and her husband, Captain Mark Phillips, and either one of them could easily have been killed.

Quickly we wrote down a list of people to make up the murder squad and the officers we needed to call out. First we needed an experienced officer to take charge of the murder squad office, to interpret telephone calls and to be capable of making decisions. We decided on Detective Sergeant John Hefford as the right man. For our exhibits officer we chose another reliable officer, Detective Constable Robert Morgan. He had been on duty that night and had gone to the scene with Sgt Forsyth, staying on to guard the door. We decided to bring in a couple of other detectives to help with the investigation in the area at Lower Belgrave Street. We also arranged with New Scotland Yard for a photographer to visit the house to take shots of the murder scene. Although it was still dark it was important to get an accurate pictorial record at every stage. We would take no chances, even if the case looked simple enough on the face of it. We knew from experience that even the most open-and-shut case had a nasty habit of blowing up in your face. Nothing could be taken for granted and procedures would be followed to the letter.

By then the ever-alert press had got hold of the news. There was no mystery how the scribes knew about it so swiftly. Some news agencies simply monitored police radio frequencies and those of the ambulance service and fire brigade 24-hours-a-day. When we knew about something newsworthy Fleet Street's finest were hotfoot on the trail soon afterwards. Reporters and photographers were already doorstepping at Lower Belgrave Street and newsrooms were laying siege to the Press Bureau at the Yard for details. The news had broken too late to make the dailies but the evening papers were champing at the bit, sensing a headline-making scoop in the heady cocktail of murder and high society.

It was agreed I would speak to the Press Office and give them sufficient information to, hopefully, keep the hacks off our backs. I told them the basic facts and said there was a suggestion Lord Lucan was in the area at the time and that we were looking for him. I stressed that because we were dealing with the aristocracy there would obviously be a lot of interest in the case. I was deliberately guarded, aware once I told the Press Bureau something and they had written it down I might have to answer for it to a sharp defence lawyer at a subsequent hearing at the Old Bailey. A spokesman told the media with masterly understatement: 'We are trying to trace Lord Lucan to tell him of the incident.'

It was important, too, that Roy should immediately inform both the Divisional CID Commander and the Divisional Commander so they could alert the Metropolitan Commissioner on what was happening. By then the news-hounds would be ringing up their tame MPs to get information, Whitehall always leaked like a sieve, and if we weren't quick off the mark a blaze of misinformation would be raging that would be difficult to control. If the Commissioner was asked and knew nothing about what was going on he would rightly have cause for complaint. We would be in the firing line.

2 The House of Horror

Number 46 Lower Belgrave Street is a five-storey building, white stuccoed to the first floor with bare brickwork above. A pair of French windows on the first floor lead from a drawing room and study onto a balcony with some fancy black-painted wrought ironwork. At pavement level there are spiked railings and steps lead up to the front door with an arch of glass over the top matching the adjacent window on the raised first floor. It is a typical mid-terrace house of the Regency period, much bigger and rambling on the inside that it appears from the outside. At the time of the murder the bedrooms of the children and their nanny were on the top floor with the nursery below on the third floor. Lady Lucan's bedroom was on the second floor with an adjoining bathroom. I knew before we arrived that the first officers on the scene had found a blood-stained towel lying on her pillow on the bed.

Our CID officer on the door gave us the bad news that I was half expecting to hear. He told us that before he took up his post there had been great activity, with uniformed officers swarming all over the house. It inevitably happens: officers make a beeline for the scene of an interesting looking crime, some thinking they might be of genuine assistance, others out of curiosity when they get the scent of a hunt. Experienced CID officers take great care not to smoke at the scene, aware they might leave a cigarette end that will have saliva on it which could be tested and lead to an identification. Detectives also walk round carefully with their hands in their pockets so as not to leave unnecessary and confusing fingerprints. Unfortunately, uniformed officers are not so cautious. As a result, in the Lucan household more than fifty sets of officers' fingerprints were found which had to be eliminated. It seemed just about everyone who was on duty that night in central London must have been along to get in on the act and have a look at the grisly scene.

My first impression on entering the house was that it was dingy and dark with a number of light bulbs not working. Lady Lucan had apparently not replaced bulbs when they burned out to demonstrate she was being economical. Apart from that the house was totally ordinary, not exactly what I was expecting from the home of a lord and lady. There were some pictures of illustrious ancestors staring from the walls, but no coronets in display cabinets, no valuable antiques or *objet d'art*, nothing at all to show it was the town residence of a peer of the realm. The furniture had mostly seen better days and the decoration was old. Unlike other Belgravia houses I had visited there were no modern appliances in the kitchen and the shower in the bathroom was equally old-fashioned. Overall the feeling I got was of faded elegance. It wasn't like a family house at all, no knick-knacks, oddly cold and bleak, not homely at all. At that time I did not know the full extent of Lucan's feud with his wife over custody of their children and the crippling financial problems that drove him to plot to kill her.

As we entered the house through the front door the dining room was on our left through double doors. At the back of the narrow hall were four steps leading down to a cloakroom at the end of a landing with a cupboard along the side. Before the cloakroom was a door under the main staircase with eight more steps going down to a kitchen at the front of the house and a breakfast room with French windows leading into a small back garden surrounded by a high brick wall with a trellis on top. The breakfast room was sparsely furnished with a round table, bookshelves beside a fireplace and an upright piano. When we went down into the basement it was in darkness. Some light entered from a street lamp outside, through the slats of a half-open venetian blind on the kitchen window, but we relied on emergency lighting from heavy-duty torches taken from the police radio van. There was a ceiling light with a shade hanging over the foot of the stairs. The bulb was missing, taken out of its socket and left lying on one of the chairs. I hoped the 100 watt bulb was untouched by any of the uniformed officers who had trampled through the kitchen as it could have important fingerprints on it. Whoever had taken out the bulb was probably the killer, wanting to lurk under the cloak of darkness waiting for his victim. The only other light came from the glowing red bulb of a kettle on the worktop in the kitchen.

With the light from my torch I could see heavy blood-stains on the carpet on the landing and the steep stairs leading down to the basement. In the breakfast room below, blood had sprayed across the piano and the bookcase right across the room. I could see there were many tadpole-shaped splashes on the walls and ceiling. From these a forensic expert would be able to determine the distance and direction from which the blood had spurted. Between the bottom of the stairs and the kitchen was a canvas bag with 'US Mail' stencilled on it, a large sort of kitbag which you see hanging on hooks in mail rooms to sort the post. It was standing upright against the wall, top open, cords not pulled together. There was a woman's arm hanging out of it with a small gold watch on the wrist. The mail-bag was surrounded by a pool of blood about half the size of a kitchen table top. Blood had soaked from the body through the sack and spread out onto the parquet floor. Somebody had walked in the dark puddle and left a trail of footprints. A pair of black high-heeled shoes had been placed neatly beside the bag. I was used to seeing violent death, horribly mutilated murder victims, but there was something eerie about the blood-stained sack with the white arm sticking grotesquely out of it in the harsh beam of my torch.

At that time forensic had not been called, the murder scene would remain secure until it could be properly examined in the light of day. The divisional police surgeon, Dr Michael Smith, had earlier certified the woman was dead, but he had been careful not to disturb the lifeless body in doing so. There were broken cups and saucers on the floor, a picture on the stairway wall at an angle and one of the wrought iron banister rails broken. It was evident some act of shocking violence had taken place. To determine exactly what we would need to speak to Lady Lucan.

The first time I saw Lady Lucan she was propped up on pillows in a bed at St George's Hospital, looking pale and very weak. A policeman was sitting at her bedside. It was about 2 a.m. and we had driven straight to the hospital from her home. A great wedge of her scalp was missing. Her ugly injuries had not been bandaged but they weren't bleeding. Her hair was thickly matted with blood and she was still wearing a sapphire necklace. I don't think at that stage she had been x-rayed to determine if the blows to her head had damaged her skull. She looked small and frail, like an injured bird. We had been told by the medical staff we could see her but only for a short time. We were not looking to take a formal statement. There would be plenty of time for that later when she was feeling better. All we really needed to know now was the identity of the man who had attacked her. She was very drowsy, I assumed as a result of sedatives the casualty department might have administered. Her injuries looked extremely painful.

Roy Ranson introduced himself, then introduced me.

'Does that hurt very much?' he asked gently, receiving a nod in reply. 'I'm sorry. Can you tell us, in your own words, what happened?'

Speaking slowly and not very coherently, with breaks between her words, she gave us our first account of the events that night – how she had been attacked by her husband, how she had fought with him and how he had told her he had killed Sandra.

'Are the children allright?' she asked weakly.

'Yes,' Roy answered. 'They are safe with their grandmother.'

'Have you found him?'

'We are looking for him. Is there anyone you would like us to tell?'

'No,' she said.

'Go to sleep now,' said Roy.

The duty doctor at the casualty department, Dr Neil Scott, the nursing sister Jennifer Gardner and staff nurse Susan Ellison had also been told by Lady Lucan that it was her husband who had attacked her and killed the nanny. And she had related the same story to her own family doctor, Dr Christopher Powell-Brett, when he saw her at St George's. It was clear Lord Lucan was the man we wanted to interview.

By the time we got back to Gerald Road there had been a dramatic development. Lord Lucan had made the second of two telephone calls to his 75-year-old mother, the Dowager Countess, at her home at Lord's View in St John's Wood. Unfortunately he had declined to speak to PC Baddick who was with her at the flat, saying he would talk to the police in the morning and ring her again. We were happily satisfied at the time that he would turn up, most probably in the company of his solicitor. In the office there was a sweepstake on what time the call would come through from the front desk to say they had arrived downstairs. Like most of the squad I thought it would happen at about 9.30 a.m., though a wag pointed out with some element of logic it would more likely be at noon because aristocrats weren't renowned as early risers.

Despite our confidence that Lord Lucan would walk through the door exactly as he said, there was still a great deal of work to be done. It was no good saying to ourselves, 'OK, at nine o'clock he'll be in, everything solved.' We had to follow procedures in exactly the same way whether he did or did not keep the promise he made to his mother on the phone. If he did turn up there was no guarantee he would confess to the crime. He could just as easily say: 'I didn't commit the murder, I was 200 miles away at the time' or 'Sorry, don't know anything about it, I was drunk as a skunk.' To presume otherwise would be very silly, so we sat down and made a list of all the things that had to be done: photographs at the scene and of the injuries to Lady Lucan, a detailed forensic examination. By then Lucan's car, a blue two-year-old Mercedes, had been found outside his rented flat at 72a Elizabeth Street, not far from Gerald Road, and had been taken away for close inspection. Two constables were stationed inside the flat in case Lord Lucan returned.

We knew the flat at Elizabeth Street was were Lord Lucan was living. The mews property he leased at 5 Eaton Row was being lived in by a banker friend, Greville Howard. Sgt Forsyth had broken into the flat and found it empty. We thought we should pay a visit, more to be nosey than anything else, to see if it would yield any clues to where he might be while we awaited his arrival and to get an impression of the man. It was about 3 a.m. when we got there.

The flat was in the basement of a property typical of that part of London. It was large and, like the house at Lower Belgrave Street, cold and sparsely furnished. The lounge was bare with no pictures on the walls, but it had a piano and a small table with slots built under it which contained bottles of spirits. There were a number of LP records, a mixture of classical recordings and modern jazz. There were also a number of reel-to-reel tapes and cassettes which I thought might be interesting. Lucan evidently wasn't bookish. Apart from some detective novels, there were some volumes on mental illness and psychiatry and some on pre-war Nazi Germany. The flat was generally bare, only an ermine robe in one of the rooms giving an indication of the occupier. Unfortunately there was no answering machine attached to the telephone and no note saying: 'Cancel the milk. I'm going away for a couple of weeks.'

What I did find which interested me was a pile of bills on the sideboard, final demands in red. Some of the brown envelopes hadn't been touched, the sign of a person who has given up even bothering to open them. Hello, I thought, something isn't right here for a titled man of substance. There were also a number of address books which I quickly thumbed through and found to be a catalogue of aristocratic names I had seen in newspaper gossip columns. His passport was in a drawer so, even if he failed to keep his morning appointment, he would have difficulty leaving the country by the official channels. In the bedroom we made the most interesting discovery. Laid out on the double bed was a suit, shirt and tie. There was a book about Greek shipping millionaires and the bedcover was strewn with a jumble of loose change, a wallet and car keys. It looked as thought everything had been tipped on the bed by someone who had emptied their pockets, gone into the bathroom and was about to return to dress. At the time the articles spread out on the bed struck us as odd, but we didn't appreciate the significance until later.

We left everything as we had found it in the flat, together with the constables who awaited the return of Lucan, passing the long hours watching his TV and tinkling on his piano.

At 10 a.m. I was at the Westminster Mortuary with Roy Ranson and DC Bob Morgan for the post-mortem, conducted by eminent Home Office pathologist Professor Keith Simpson. He was a top pathologist who in his long career had worked on a number of sensational cases. They included the A6 Murder, when James Hanratty shot Michael Gregson in a Bedfordshire lay-by and raped and crippled his girlfriend Valerie Storie, acid bath murderer John Haigh, and sadistic Neville Heath, who mutilated Margery Gardner in a Notting Hill Gate hotel. All three went to the scaffold and were hanged for their crimes. Professor Simpson had also carried out the autopsy on George Cornell, shot between the eyes by Ronnie Kray in the Blind Beggar public house in Whitechapel in March 1966.

It was important at an early stage to determine that Sandra

Rivett died as a result of a violent act and not from natural causes. She had been taken to the mortuary for the autopsy still in the mail-bag in which I had first seen her in the breakfast room. The sack was photographed before she was removed and, when she was taken out, she was photographed again fully clothed in a blood-stained flowered dress. Her clothes were then removed and handed to DC Morgan before the pathologist went about his task of determining the cause of death. Various samples were taken and given to DC Morgan for bagging, labelling and examination at the Metropolitan Police Scientific Laboratory at Lambeth. I could see for myself the only serious injuries to the body appeared to be to the head, with heavy bruising to the tops of her shoulders and some lesser bruising to her right arm and hand.

Professor Simpson confirmed death had resulted from severe blunt head injuries, three to the face and at least six to her scalp. Her skull had not been fractured but the brain was bruised and there had been considerable bleeding into her throat and windpipe. Death would have come within a minute or two because in an unconscious state she would be unable to clear the air passages by coughing. The bruising to the shoulders had evidently resulted from the rain of blows to the head that had missed their mark, that to the back of the right hand when it was raised in a futile protective gesture. A line of bruises on the top of the right arm were thought to be where a hand had gripped her tightly. Professor Simpson was shown the 9-inch long length of lead pipe bound in surgical plaster tape found at the scene and he confirmed the weapon could have caused the injuries. The autopsy did not reveal any sign of a sexual attack or of recent sexual intercourse. At 2.40 p.m. Sandra Rivett's estranged husband, Roger Rivett, attended and identified the body as that of his wife.

When we got back from the post-mortem Sgt Forsyth went to St George's Hospital to start taking a full statement from Veronica Lucan, a process that was to continue for several days with frequent breaks because she was weak from the battering she had received. Sgt Forsyth was an old stager; he knew you can't hurry people and he realized the importance of getting everything written down in the right sequence. We decided to go over and see how he was getting along. It was also a courtesy call on Lady Lucan, to tell her that everything possible was being done to find her husband and to assure her she was in safe hands.

When we arrived she was still propped up in bed but cleaned up and with her wounds now stitched and bandaged. She was an elfin-like figure, looking very pale. Naturally we asked her if she had any idea where her husband might be. When she replied 'Your guess is as good as mine', I believed her. After all, there was no reason why she should know and she was sedated, her mind still in a whirl from the traumatic events of the night. If I expected her to say 'I'm frightened he might come back and attack me', she never mentioned it. We didn't stay long, confident Sgt Forsyth would get from her all the information we needed about the assault and the state of her marriage. There were rumours the marriage was in turmoil and we wanted details.

By lunchtime on Friday it was already clear that Lord Lucan was not going to show. The *Evening Standard* was on the street with a front page headline proclaiming BELGRAVIA MURDER AT EARL'S HOME and a strapline *Body in Sack ... Countess Runs Out Screaming*. There were head-and-shoulder pictures of Lord Lucan and Lady Lucan, with a ghoulish photo on page 2 taken during the night, showing the sack containing the body of Sandra Revitt being carried down the steps.

The single-column picture of Lord Lucan was the first newspaper photograph I saw of the face that was to haunt my dreams. It showed a man with raffish good looks and a somewhat arrogant expression. He was dressed immaculately in what looked like morning dress so it was probably a photograph taken on his wedding day and dug from the files. His dark hair was slicked back and he was sporting a droopy sort of moustache much in vogue in Edwardian times. I was pleased. With his military bearing he looked totally at odds with the current fashion for long hair and trendy clothes. He would stand out like a sore thumb in a crowd and be easy to spot now his photo was staring out from TV screens and newspapers across the country.

The accompanying story said murder squad detectives were anxious to interview 39-year-old Lord Lucan in case he could give information about a nanny found beaten to death at his Belgravia home. The barman at the Plumbers Arms, Derrick

Whitehouse, was extensively quoted about Lady Lucan staggering into his bar.

An 'All Ports Warning' was put in force at seaports and airports, instructing Special Branch officers that Lord Lucan was wanted for interview. I didn't expect it to produce results. He was hardly likely to turn up at Garwick for a package tour to Spain and there were plenty of tiny harbours and airfields that weren't covered by Metropolitan Police officers. Interpol London also sent a message to Interpol Europe in Paris to put him on their 'Red Alert' register of people wanted for questioning who were either known or suspected of being abroad. The hunt for Lord Lucan had begun in earnest. But who exactly was our quarry and what had driven him to take such drastic action?

3 Bad Day at Balaclava

My copy of *Who's Who* read: 'LUCAN, 7th Earl of, *cr* 1795; Richard John Bingham; Bt 1632; Baron Lucan, 1776; Baron Bingham (UK)1934; *b* 18 Dec. 1934; *e s* of 6th Earl of Lucan, MC; *S* father 1964; *m* 1963, Veronica, *d* of late Major C.M. Duncan, MC and of Mrs J.D. Margrie; one *s* two *d. Educ*: Eton. Lieut (Res. of Officers) Coldstream Guards. *Heir: s* Lord Bingham.' Translated, it meant Lord Lucan's name was Richard John Bingham. As the eldest son of the 6th Earl, he had succeeded his father on his death in 1964. He had been married the previous year to Veronica Duncan and had three children.

Apart from the title of 7th Earl of Lucan, he also held the baronies of Melcombe Bingham in Dorset and Castlebar in the Irish Republic, all entitling him to a seat in the House of Lords, but he was yet to make his maiden speech. The family motto in Latin was *Spes Mea Christus*, which meant 'In Christ lies my hope', and the crest showed two wolves chained as protectors to a shield and an earl's coronet. The crest was appropriately topped by a falcon, hunting bird of the nobility. This time it was the holder of the peerages who had flown away and become the quarry.

Further investigation revealed Lucan was descended from an old West Country family. His ancestors could be traced back to the thirteenth century when one Robert de Bingham became Bishop of Salisbury in 1229, beginning a tradition of public life that was to continue through the centuries. The family had served many kings and queens and it was even said there was royal blood in the bloodline through an illegitimate child of King Charles II. Interestingly, one of his ancestors had become the Countess Spencer, though at that time it was of little significance to me as Diana was only a young girl and yet to marry Prince Charles and become the Princess of Wales.

The long Lucan association with western Ireland began when three adventurous Bingham brothers bought land four centuries ago and built up vast estates in County Mayo, a Captain John Bingham buying a castle at Castlebar. They had been soldiers of fortune and the family acquired a reputation for ruthlessness. Sir Richard Bingham, the governor of Connaught, had blood on his hands as a result of a particularly callous act. He ordered the massacre of the crews of two big ships from the Spanish Armada driven ashore by a gale on 10 September 1588, and the butchered sailors and soldiers are buried at a place now called Spanish Point on the Loop Head peninsula. The title of Baron of Lucan of Castlebar was given to Charles Bingham in 1776 by George II, and in 1795 he became the Earl of Lucan by royal favour.

Like all schoolboys who grew up when atlases were painted the pink of British Empire and history was high on the classroom curriculum, I knew the story of Lucan's great-great-grandfather in the Crimean War. The 3rd Earl of Lucan was held responsible for one of the worst military disasters in history, the loss of the Light Brigade at Balaclava. I had learned the immortal verses of Alfred Tennyson's heroic poem *The Charge of the Light Brigade* and lines from it were still familiar: 'Half a league, half a league, half a league onward, All in the valley of Death, Rode the six hundred ... Cannon to right of them, Cannon to left of them, Cannon in front of them, Volley'd and thunder'd.' Patriotic stuff, the Poet Laureate cleverly turning a spectacular blunder that wiped out the cream of the British cavalry at Balaclava into a stunning public relations triumph that would endure for ever.

What interested me was what the calamity might tell us about the personality of the 3rd Earl of Lucan. He was known to have a violent temper, and that may have been a contributory factor in giving the fatal order to charge the Russian guns, an action which he knew full well was futile. It is arguable he was not to blame at all, having received muddled or badly written orders from Lord Raglan, the Commander-in-Chief, as to the valley in which the attack should be lauched. But if Lord Lucan, the Commander of the Cavalry Division, had lost his head in fury and acted recklessly it could be a family trait worth noting. Exactly 120 years later there were clear signs emerging that the 7th Earl of Lucan had similarly panicked when faced with a crisis, causing his sanity and rationality to desert him.

Certainly the 3rd Earl carried the can for the débâcle in the valley of death, being denied the court-martial he demanded that might have cleared his name for giving the fatal order: 'Forward, the Light Brigade!' He became the scapegoat, dubbed 'Lord Look-On', for the insane charge that resulted in 102 soldiers being killed, 127 wounded and another 58 captured. Meanwhile, his brother-in-law who led the charge, Lord Cardigan, survived and emerged a hero, the mob that had once abused him turning to a cheering crowd. He had been nicknamed 'the Noble Yachtsman' for living on a luxury yacht while his soldiers faced cholera and typhus in squalor in freezing conditions ashore, and he was held in total contempt by Lord Lucan. The Earl of Cardigan was recognized as a man with no military experience, ill suited to the command he had purchased, whereas Lord Lucan earned his spurs on the field of battle and was regarded as highly intelligent. Lord Lucan married Lord Cardigan's sister Anne in 1829 and the two men held a deep hatred for one another, maintaining a feud throughout the war. It was yet another side of Lucan's character I would soon learn seemed to have echoes in the behaviour of his great-great-grandson.

But it was in the 3rd Earl's life years before his disgrace at Balaclava that I was to discover the greatest pointers to his character. He had entered the army as a youth of sixteen and bought the command of the 17th Lancers for £25,000 in 1826, remaining as their Lieutenant-Colonel until 1837. Before he succeeded to the title in 1839 he went to Ireland when he left his regiment two years earlier to manage the family estates. His intention was to raise more money from his farms because, like other mostly absentee English landowners, the estates were seen only as a source of revenue. The welfare of the tenants was not a consideration and in County Mayo they were poor even by destitute Irish standards, living in miserable huts alongside their animals and relying for food on the potato crops in order to survive. When the crops failed in four successive years from 1845 to 1848, Lord Lucan evicted his tenant families to starve to death in ditches, tearing down their pitiful shelters and even closing the doors of the workhouse at Castlebar so many more died. Called on to explain his heartless actions in the House of Lords, he answered with chilling logic that the tenants hadn't paid their rates so he could not pay for providing them with relief.

It was hardly surprising Lord Lucan was one of the most hated men in Ireland, earning the nickname of 'the Exterminator' for the harsh treatment of his tenants. Yet, ironically, it was these ruthless qualities and total disregard for public opinion that probably led to his being given command of the Cavalry Division when the British Army embarked on their ill-fated mission to the Crimea.

Having sullied the long and distinguished Lucan military tradition in twenty minutes of needless slaughter in a hail of Russian bullets and shells, the 3rd Earl lived on to become the oldest soldier in the British Army and died at the ripe old age of ninety-three. By the time of his death in 1888 George Bingham was a respected senior member of the House of Lords, his tarnished reputation somewhat restored, while that of Lord Cardigan had declined. Lord Lucan was made a field-marshal on Queen Victoria's Jubilee and his body was carried at his funeral on a gun carriage with full military escort.

Apart from his wicked temper Lord Lucan had shown himself to be a man of little sentiment, both aggressive and paranoid, believing his intentions to be entirely worthy and misunderstood by those who sought to criticize. He was arrogantly self-confident and self-righteous too, trying and failing to abolish the Queen's court in Castlebar in order to dispense his own brand of law on the local populace. If the man we were now hunting, the 7th Earl, exhibited some of the fierce qualities possessed by his cruel Victorian predecessor he was going to be a formidable and cunning adversary. An oil paintings of Lord Lucan, resplendent in dress uniform, showed a tall, athletic-looking man, not dissimilar facially to his descendant. He posed with his hand firmly on the hilt of his sabre and didn't look the sort of man who would readily unsheathe it from its scabbard and fall on the blade when the going got tough.

I guessed that Lucan, as a child, would certainly have been taught by heart all the verses of Tennyson's stirring poem about the thundering mile-and-a-half ride of the glorious Light Brigade into the history books. I wondered if he was as familiar with *Maud*, the equally famous tragic love poem Tennyson wrote and published at the same time as *The Charge of the Light Brigade*. It is a morbid tale of hereditary madness and melancholia, of a society sick with wealth, family feud, bankruptcy and killing, its neurotic hero finally going off to face what looks like suicidal death in the Crimea. Tennyson denied, unconvincingly, that the poem mirrored his own early life, and it struck me there were parallels with the 'black blood' in bygone generations of the Lucan family. One line from *Maud* came to mind as I recalled the gruesome scene in the basement at No. 46 Lower Belgrave Street: *'The red-ribbed ledges drip with a silent horror of blood.'*

The failure of Lucan to keep his appointment prompted us to look carefully at exactly what he had said in his two telephone calls to his mother, the Dowager Lady Kaitilin Lucan, known as Kait. She had twice spoken on the telephone to her son after the murder, the first time when he asked her to go to No. 46 to remove the children and the second time after she returned home to her flat, inquiring about them and saying he would call the police in the morning.

Kait had arrived at No. 46 to find the house filled with policemen. She was interviewed in the dining room by Sgt Forsyth, who had arrived a couple of minutes later and informed her that Veronica had been attacked and was in hospital and that the nanny was dead. It wasn't a formal interview but Sgt Forsyth had made notes of the conversation in his pocketbook, a sensible precaution because Kait was to query later exactly what she said.

Kait had apparently returned to her flat from a meeting and had answered the telephone at about 10.45 p.m. The caller said it was John speaking and he had sounded very shocked, as if knocked for six, his words stumbling out.

'There has been a terrible catastrophe at No. 46,' he had said. 'Veronica is hurt and I want you to collect the children as quickly as possible. Ring Bill Shand Kydd immediately.' Bill Shand Kydd, Sgt Forsyth explained, was an old friend of Lucan's and his brother-in-law through marriage to Veronica's sister Christina.

Lucan had also said to her that the nanny had been hurt. When she had asked 'Badly?' he replied: 'Yes, I think so.'

In the conversation Lucan had been incoherent but had said he had been driving past the house when he had seen a fight going on in the basement between Veronica and a man. He had gone in and joined them and the man ran off. Veronica was shouting and screaming. There was blood and mess in the basement. He had tried to clean Veronica up.

According to Sgt Forsyth, Lucan had said to the Dowager Countess: 'Oh, mother, there was something terrible in the basement. I couldn't bring myself to look.'

When Kait had pressed him for more details Lucan had repeated that she should get the children out. She had asked who would let her in to No. 46 and he said he supposed Frances.

When she had asked: 'Where are you going?' Lucan had replied 'I don't know' and had rung off.

In the second conversation with Lucan, at 12.30 a.m. after Kait had collected the children and put them to bed in her flat, her son had been calmer and more rational, 'more on all fours' as she colloquially put it.

'Have you got the children?' he asked her.

'They are all safe here in the flat and asleep,' she replied.

'That's all right then.'

Kait told him the police were in the flat and asked him if he wanted to speak to PC Baddick. The constable had been beside her but, unfortunately, had not taken the phone from her to speak to Lucan.

Lucan said to Kait: 'No, I think not now. I'll ring them in the morning and ring you, too.'

Kait had put down the telephone and said to the constable: 'That was my son. He won't speak to you now. He'll phone you in the morning.'

There was nothing in the conversations as reported to us to give any indication of where Lucan was going or where he had been when he made the phone calls. What was interesting was that Kait had said there were no 'ticks' on the line indicating a pay phone, nor was a telephone operator involved. The calls had both been made from private telephones.

In her interview with Sgt Forsyth, the Dowager Countess said Lucan and his wife were separated. Their children had been made wards of court and Veronica had custody. She also gave the first indication of the deep feud between the two and the battle over custody of their three children.

'He's separated,' she told Sgt Forsyth. 'The children were made wards of court and Veronica was told to continue with medical treatment for her mental complaint.'

'What was that?' he asked her.

'Manic-depressive, not violent, except verbally,' she replied.

'In the original court case it was thought she was a danger to the children.'

That was our first intimation that we were not dealing with a normal domestic conflict but a complex case with a history of hostility centred on custody of the children. There was also some information in the interview that we now already knew: that Lucan owned the mews cottage at 5 Eaton Row, that he himself lived in a flat nearby at 72a Elizabeth Street, and that his car was a blue Mercedes. The car had been found parked opposite the flat, its engine cold. When Sgt Forsyth had broken into the flat through a rear window it was, not surprisingly, empty with no sign of Lucan.

Now Lucan had failed to show up his mother would need to be interviewed again to see if there was anything she might have missed out that could give a clue to his whereabouts. I looked forward to meeting her; from all accounts she sounded quite a character.

When Michael Stoop, a retired company director and old backgammon-playing friend of Lucan, heard the police were looking for him he got in touch with us. 'I lent him my car,' he said. 'Where is it? Have you got it?' The news that Lucan had been loaned a car was an important lead. We already had possession of Lucan's Mercedes and had no idea how he might be travelling without it. Michael Stoop made a statement saying he had lent his car, a battered old Ford, to Lucan a fortnight before, on 21 or 23 October, after a conversation at the *Portland Club*. He had offered to loan Lucan his own Mercedes but he said he wanted to borrow the banger. Lucan hadn't said why he wanted it but he did not ask for a reason. He knew his friend was having trouble with his wife, and he was under the impression he wanted the car to keep her under observation in a vehicle that would not attract her attention. He left the keys in the car outside the garage for Lucan to collect it. A description of the car – a dark blue Ford Corsair, index number KYN 135D – was immediately circulated to police forces throughout the country.

4 The Warrior Breed

If ever there was a man born with silver spoons jangling in his mouth but hopelessly out of his time it was self-indulgent Lord Lucan. He was known to his friends as John or Johnny, but called simply Lucan by us for the sake of brevity. He would have fitted happily into an earlier age as the quintessential Englishman, a Regency buck or an Edwardian toff, when the upper crust ruled as if by divine right and led an enviable life of moneyed privilege. Lucan would have been regarded as a born leader of men, so it was perhaps unfortunate that in the 1950s there were no 'decent' wars going on. National Service, two years of time-wasting drudgery, was all that was on offer for the 18-year-old Lucan when he left school and received his 'call up' papers in 1953.

There was, of course, the patronage to which he was already accustomed in that he was able to waltz straight into the Coldstream Guards. His father, Patrick 'Pat' Bingham, the 6th Earl, had commanded the 1st Battalion of the Coldstream Guards in the Second World War and this provided the entrée. While other conscripts sat in the Libyan sand or acted as guinea-pigs for atom bomb tests on far off Christmas Island young Lucan, fresh from Eaton Hall Officers' Cadet School with his commission as a 2nd lieutenant, was given what was considered a prime posting to West Germany to join the 2nd Battalion stationed at Krefeld. He would have preferred to have stayed in England for the social life enjoyed by other blue bloods. But Germany wasn't a bad posting, even if the natives were somewhat resentful at receiving their second drubbing and there were fears any day the Russian tanks would burst through the Iron Curtain or lob over an atom bomb or two.

National Service passed pleasantly enough, offering plenty of opportunity for sport for the athletic Lucan and friendly

Switzerland close at hand for some bobsleighing and fun *après-ski*. But it wasn't the shooting, tennis or winter sports that were his main pastime. Like thousands of other reluctant soldiers, he whiled away boring hours in barracks playing cards. Unlike the other ranks who risked their lowly pay playing brag, bridge and poker were played in the officer's mess for stakes on the turn of a card that would have kept a sprog on 42-shillings-a-week in clover. There were occasional sorties, too, to a casino at Bad Neuenahr, early signs of a love affair with the seductive green baize tables.

Lucan's addiction to gambling first began as a teenager at Eton, Britain's top public school, and was eventually to take over his life and lead to his downfall. At Eton, where he was a pupil from the age of thirteen after leaving a preparatory school in Oxfordshire, he was a house captain in his final year. Otherwise his schooldays were largely undistinguished, apart from awakening a love of classical music and an illicit introduction to fickle Lady Luck. He risked expulsion by playing cards and taking bets to supplement his pocket-money and got into trouble visiting racecourses. At Eton he built up a coterie of loyal friends who shared his passion for gambling and a buccaneering spirit that made them determined to cock a snook at what they saw as a hidebound society.

Prep schools and the playing fields of Eton gave the young Lucan the indefinable style and polish that separates the aristocracy from the common herd. But it was in America that he developed an appreciation of how wealth provides the key to enjoying the finer things of life. With his brother and two sisters he was evacuated to the safety of the United States as a 5-year-old early in the war as German bombs rained down on London in the blitz and threatened the family home at 22 Eaton Square. To those less advantaged children tearfully packed off with labels tied around their necks, evacuation wasn't perhaps the right word for avoiding the privations of war-time Britain. After staying briefly in Wales he sailed on a liner to Canada in 1940, moved on to America and spent the war years living under the protection of a hugely rich woman named Mrs Margaret Brady Tucker who owned property in New York and Florida. Known to the children as Aunt Marcia, she was able to attend to their needs with a governess, butler and cook in their own house in the grounds of a summer mansion she owned called

Penwood, not far out of New York City at Westchester. The super-rich able to leave Britain as the Germans threatened to invade did not endear themselves to those who had to stay behind, it was said in a play on the title of the Hollywood blockbuster film showing in London they had 'Gone With The Wind Up'.

Lucan toyed with the idea of following family tradition, signing on in the Army and predictable progress up the ladder to high command. But he lacked sufficient financial backing to enjoy to the full the benefits available in the Services and the climb through the ranks would take time. For a similar financial reason Christ Church, Oxford, lacked appeal, his father refusing to provide a generous subsidy to enjoy university life in comfort in the city of dreaming spires. London promised more scope to indulge the good life as a civilian with the advantages he felt his birthright and good looks entitled him to expect. If it wasn't to be the Army there was only one place for a gentleman of breeding to work: the City. When he was demobbed Lucan was taken on by merchant bank William Brandt as a management trainee at a salary of just £500 a year, a lot less money than the thousands he would soon be winning or losing in a single evening at the gaming tables playing *chemin de fer*, backgammon and poker. At Brandt's his passion for cards was confined to playing in the bank's bridge team and he was a regular lunchtime customer in nearby Jules Bar, frustrated at not making a rapid rise to a directorship and the riches he impatiently sought.

Outside of work, Lucan, with his title and natural charm, had the time of his life in a round of debutante parties. But he was more interested in gambling and adventurous outdoor sports than the adoring debs who craved his company and coveted his title. He bobsleighed at St Moritz and was the driver of the Great Britain four-man bob that came ninth in 1957, an old friend from his Army days, Bill Shand Kydd, heir to the wallpaper fortune and amateur National Hunt jockey, in the team as his brakeman. He raced a powerful speedboat named *White Migrant* in a *Daily Express* offshore powerboat race at Cowes on the Isle of Wight, ignominiously sinking. Certainly he wasn't lacking in courage to take part in these risky sports, so he didn't seem the sort of man who would shirk at carrying out a cold-blooded murder with his bare hands.

Lucan also waterskiied and played golf to a handicap of fourteen and he enjoyed both sports on frequent trips abroad to the playgrounds of Europe. Usually there was a casino to hand, illegal at the time in Britain. At home Lucan had to rely on illegal gambling. His friend John Aspinall, who he met in 1954, ran the most upmarket of the floating games that operated in Mayfair with constant changes of address. It wasn't only upper class gambling pursuits he enjoyed, like flying to France in a private plane for a weekend at Deauville racecourse and playing roulette and baccarat in the casino at Le Touquet. He enjoyed horse racing, the sport of kings, and at one time owned a horse prophetically called *Stress Signal*. He wasn't snobby when it came to gambling, either, enjoying the cloth cap sport of dog racing and owning a greyhound named *Sambo's Hangover*.

For the children of light, the 1950s was a golden age when they were able to enjoy a lifestyle denied the working masses, not unlike the 1930s but led at a faster pace with planes replacing ships and offering quick travel to exciting locations. Their antics recorded in newspapers appeared glamorous in a country where rationing had only just been abolished and gloomy post-war austerity was a recent memory. While the rest of us in London relished the early days of rock and roll in Soho coffee bars like *The Two I*'s, the young Lucan was to be found in expensive West End clubs like the *Mandrake* and *Gargoyle*. I remembered there was much space given in the tabloid newspaper gossip columns to what was called the 'Chelsea set' and Princess Margaret's activities based on the *400 Club* made top-of-the-page news. Elopements made the news, too, two in particular involving the Lucan circle, that of Dominic Elwes and Tessa Kennedy, god-daughter of Princess Marina, and James Goldsmith with Isabel Patino, 17-year-old daughter of Bolivian tin millionaire Don Antenor Patino. Pursued by private detectives and the press, Goldsmith and Isabel ran off to Scotland and married. Isabel died later in childbirth and a battle followed with the family in the French courts for custody of the baby, which Goldsmith won.

It was inevitable that gambling was finally to take over Lucan's life. Fortune smiled on him at the tables, so much so that he was given the nickname 'Lucky' by his fellow gamblers. After a spectacular win of £26,000 in two nights playing chemmy, he decided to give up working for Brandt's and become a professional gambler, to the dismay of his parents and against the advice of his friends. The big win may have been an exaggeration, or even a total invention, an excuse to leave the bank where he felt his career wasn't making fast enough progress. Anyway, with his new found freedom and cash in his pocket he went for a long holiday to America, exploring the West Coast and the Grand Canyon in an open-top sports car. When he returned it was to a face an uncertain future in a new decade, the 1960s.

Gambling exploded with the passing of the Betting and Gaming Bill on 29 July 1960, legalizing casinos along with betting shops and bingo halls. John Aspinall opened the *Clermont Club* in Berkeley Square, which was to become the hub of Lucan's life as a gambler. It was in this exclusive and unreal atmosphere, a deliberately recreated theatrical time capsule of eighteenth century splendour, that Lucan felt entirely at home, isolated and insulated in monastic solitude in the tense silence of the gaming rooms from the changes taking place outside. In a world of long-haired hippies wearing Afghan coats over cheesecloth shirts and flared jeans, Lucan was to become an incongruous figure, his view of life as outmoded as his short-back-and-sides haircut and blue pinstripe suits.

Lucan's father, George Charles Patrick Bingham, the 6th Earl of Lucan, was born in 1898 and was educated at Eton and Sandhurst. He was commissioned in the Coldstream Guards in World War One and served with distinction, picking up a Military Cross in 1917 to partly atone for the cock-up his great-grandfather made at Balaclava. He commanded the 1st Battalion of the Coldstream Guards from 1940 to 1942 and was then Deputy Director of Ground Defence at the Air Ministry until the war ended, retiring from the Army in 1947. Dismayed by the inequality of life in post-war Britain he turned to Socialism and when his father, a former Conservative MP, died in 1949 and he succeeded to the title he straight away took the Labour Whip in the House of Lords. For a short time, between June and October 1951, he was Under-Secretary of State for Commonwealth Relations in the Labour Government, finally becoming Chief Opposition Whip in the Lords in 1954 and holding the post until his death. His wife Kaitilin, who he married in 1920, shared his political beliefs. They were both active workers for the Labour cause in the then North London constituency of Marylebone, where Kait was secretary and served on the borough council.

To the materialistic Lucan the left-wing leanings of his egalitarian parents was an embarrassing aberration. He knew his friends regarded them virtually as out-and-out communists. To make matters worse, his father opened up the family archives to writer Cecil Woodham-Smith for his book *The Reason Why*, detailing the 3rd Earl's behaviour in the Irish famine and his role at Balaclava. It was published in 1953, just as Lucan was going into the Army, and was probably the reason why he answered to the name Arthur during his National Service to try and avoid being tarred with the Lucan Crimea brush.

If his parents' vision of a society based on fair shares for all was anathema to Lucan, it was equally true his worship of the god of Mammon was repellent to them. They watched with distaste his hedonistic jet-set lifestyle, paid for not by honest sweat-of-the-brow endeavour but by one of the less appealing aspects of capitalism, gambling. They were appalled when he decided to give up work altogether and become a professional gambler.

The statement eventually produced by Sgt Forsyth from his interview with Veronica was a lengthy one, running to nine typed foolscap sheets, which meant he had probably written about twenty sheets in longhand which he would have read back to her. She would have signed each one at the bottom before he gave them to a typist who would make six copies and put them in trays for various officers. The original would be placed in the archives to be produced in court. One of the photostats was our working copy and we would make notes on it of anything that was missed out or needed further action.

Sgt Forsyth did a good job. The statement described in detail her attack on the stairs. Veronica also went into the problems of the marriage, something we knew was going to be a big side issue. Basically the statement confirmed what we already knew. Veronica said her husband was her assailant. That got the big tick from the felt tip pen. What also got a mark was a discrepancy in the time between when Veronica said she was attacked and when her daughter, Lady Frances, had verbally told Sgt Forsyth her mother went downstairs looking for the nanny. Frances said it happened before the *Nine O'Clock News* started on BBC1, whereas it was getting on for ten o'clock before Veronica burst into the Plumbers Arms screaming blue murder. What had happened during the long period in between? I wasn't all that bothered. Time is a funny thing in murder inquiries, and people have different ideas about it. In most inquiries timing is terrible, people can't remember time even though they think they can. The timing was marked on the working copy as needing tightening up but no great significance was attached to it.

In her statement Veronica said she was lying on her bed in her bedroom on the second floor and had watched *Mastermind* on television. She was with her daughter Frances and, shortly before nine o'clock, Sandra had put her head around the bedroom door and asked if she wanted a cup of tea, taking with her a tray of dirty crockery. Veronica watched the nine o'clock news until 9.15, at which point she wondered what had happened to Sandra and went looking for her on the ground floor. It was dark in the hallway because the light bulbs had burned out and not been replaced. At the top of the staircase leading to the basement kitchen she saw the light in the basement was off and was puzzled because she realized Sandara couldn't be making tea in the dark.

Veronica continued that she had called out 'Sandra ... Sandra'. Then, behind her, she heard a rustling sound from the cloakroom and was struck at least four blows on the right side of her head. She didn't fall down but struggled and screamed out. Her attacker thrust gloved fingers down her throat and said 'Shut up', at which point she realized that her assailant was her husband. She continued to put up a fight and he tried to strangle her and gouged her left eye with his thumb. They fell into the basement stairway and she pushed the first banister rail out of position with her leg. After she grabbed his testicles her husband appeared to lose his strength. She remembered sitting between his legs while he sat on one of the four steps in the hall leading down to the landing, breathing heavily.

The statement related how, after fighting for her life, Veronica engaged in a battle of wits with her exhausted husband. She had asked: 'Where is my nanny?' and he had replied: 'She's gone out.' When she argued that Sandra wouldn't have gone out he said: 'She is dead.' Realizing she had to play for time she had told him: 'Oh, dear, what shall we do with the body?' and he had said: 'She is downstairs, but don't look. It is a horrid sight, an awful mess.' Despite the pain of her injuries Veronica had pretended to be helpful and Lucan had taken her up to her bedroom. Frances was still watching TV and was told to go to her bedroom. Veronica said she wanted to lie down on the bed and, when he had gone into the bathroom to get a cloth to clean her injuries, she seized on the opportunity, jumping up and running down the stairs out into the street.

Most of the facts of the attack on Veronica we already knew before they were committed to paper. What was interesting was that Veronica said Thursday was normally the nanny's day off but, that week, Sandra had asked to switch it to the Wednesday. It looked like we were dealing with a case of mistaken identity.

At 11.30 p.m. I left the office. I had been awake for a straight forty hours, most of it at work, and I was dog tired. I drove home with an uneasy feeling. What had seemed a fairly cut-and-dried case was showing signs of being a lot more complicated than it first appeared.

5 Family at War

On Saturday morning the murder squad office was in full swing. It was a room about 20 ft by 15 ft, with a square of desks closely arranged around that of office manager Sgt John Hefford so an interchange of information could easily take place. On a separate desk were a number of telephones with outside lines installed by the General Post Office. They were already humming, as were those on the other desks attached to the switchboard downstairs. Portable blackboards had written on them in coloured chalk the names of the officers on the case and where they were, messages for them and important things to be done. Typists in an outer office were busy transcribing written statements. The day's newspapers were on a desk waiting for cuttings to be taken and stuck in a book. Photographs of Lucan were already pinned up on a board.

In any major inquiry it is important to keep the troops informed of what is going on. Regular briefings are held for a variety of reasons, not least to keep up morale if the hunt is going cold. Apathy can easily creep in, resulting in little or no work getting done. On that morning enthusiasm was high as Roy Ranson and I held a meeting for everyone who was on duty. We gave them an update on the situation and told them what we knew about Sandra Rivett and the results of the post-mortem examination.

Already house-to-house inquiries were well under way in the area of Belgravia surrounding Lucan's three properties. Officers were knocking on doors, asking residents if they had seen anything untoward and were questioning milkmen, postmen and other people making deliveries. We weren't too hopeful it would produce anything worthwhile, as the filthy weather on Thursday night would have kept most people indoors. The importance of house-to-house inquiries isn't only to get a positive result, however, it is to provide protection at a subsequent court case. If a smart defence lawyer suddenly pulled out of the hat an eye-witness living nearby, we could produce a detective to refute the testimony. Our witness could say that the person had been seen and not said anything at the time.

At one house visited by a detective he explained to the elderly woman resident the purpose of his call, telling her gently how Sandra Rivett had been killed. 'Oh, dear,' she responded sorrowfully, 'nannies are so hard to get nowadays.'

Immediately after the briefing I was in my office with Roy Ranson when the phone rang. The caller said he was Bill Shand Kydd, brother-in-law of Lucan.

'I've received two letters,' he said. 'They are from John, I recognize his writing. What shall I do with them?'

'Bring them to the police station,' Roy told him, 'and don't open them.'

Bill Shand Kydd arrived at Gerald Road at about 9.30 a.m., bringing with him two envelopes. They were both ordinary little ones of the type used for private correspondence. On the backs of them were what looked like smears of blood.

Roy Ranson carefully slit them open, wearing plastic gloves, and together we read the contents. One of them said:

Dear Bill,
    The most ghastly circumstances arose tonight which I briefly described to my mother. When I interrupted the fight at Lower Belgrave St and when the man left Veronica accused me of having hired him. I took her upstairs and sent Frances up to bed and tried to clean her up. She lay doggo for a bit and when I was in the bathroom left the house. The circumstantial evidence against me is strong in that V will say it was all my doing. I will also lie doggo for a bit but I am only concerned for the children. If you can manage it I want them to live with you. Coutts (trustees) St Martin's Lane (Mr Wall) will handle school fees. V has demonstrated her hatred for me in the past and would do anything to see me accused. For George and Frances to go through life knowing their father had stood in the dock for attempted murder would be too much. When they are old enough to understand, explain to them the dream of paranoia, and look after them.
                          Yours ever
                          John

The second letter was brief. It was headed *Financial matters* and referred to a sale coming up at Christie's on 27 November, saying it would satisfy bank overdrafts. It listed the banks where the proceeds should go and added: 'The other creditors can get lost for the time being.'

Bill Shand Kydd confirmed the spidery handwriting and signature was that of Lucan. The letters that had arrived that morning at his London home in Cambridge Square had been written by his brother-in-law. What was even more important, they had obviously been written by him after the murder. It was our first big break.

The postmarks on both letters indicated they were posted at Uckfield in Sussex. Bill Shand Kydd told us a friend of Lucan's, Ian Maxwell-Scott, lived with his wife Susan at Uckfield. They were the only people he thought Lucan knew in the Uckfield area. The only other connection Lucan had with Sussex was the fact he had been powerboat racing on the South Coast. From my knowledge of the area I knew Uckfield was only some sixteen miles from the channel port of Newhaven.

Bill Shand Kydd provided a wealth of information, the more vital because he was a relative. He was evidently highly responsible, too, having rung us immediately he received the letters without even opening them because he knew we were searching for Lucan. As an old friend of Lucan's from their Army days he had become his brother-in-law when they married two sisters, Veronica and Christina Duncan, so he knew a lot about him. He was able to tell us about the breakdown in the marriage of Lucan and his wife, appearing to take Lucan's side in the domestic issue. We already knew from what the Dowager Countess had indicated that Veronica was regarded as being mentally unstable. Bill Shand Kydd was able to tell us the full facts about the separation and the bitter tug-of-love court custody battle over their three children. At the end of an interview lasting about two hours we were beginning to get a picture of Lucan and the financial problems he was facing.

As a result of the information solicited from Bill Shand Kydd, one of our detectives was dispatched to Uckfield to speak to the Maxwell-Scotts to see if they might know anything about the whereabouts of Lucan. The 'All Ports Warning' was reissued and the police in Sussex were contacted and told that Lucan had been in their area and might have been heading for Newhaven.

They also were told to be on the lookout for Michael Stoop's battered Ford Corsair.

The letters were sent for forensic examination to have the blood smears on the envelopes analysed. It looked like they had been written by someone who had sealed them by wiping them with a bloody hand or sleeve. We mulled over the content of the main letter to see if it afforded any clues to what Lucan intended to do, but the evidence was contradictory. On the one hand he said he would 'lie doggo for a bit', but the final sentence suggested he would never see his children again. What was meant by the phrase 'dream of paranoia' was anybody's guess. Lucan was a deeply troubled man and was clearly under stress at the time he wrote the letters. When we asked Bill Shand Kydd if he thought Lucan was the sort of man who would kill himself, he said no, but, there again, he didn't think he was the sort of man who would commit murder either.

We also wondered why Lucan had posted two letters to Bill Shand Kydd when he could easily have put both in the same envelope. All we could suggest was that he had already sealed one when he had further thoughts and wrote another. There was also the question as to why he should have sent them to his brother-in-law as distinct from anyone else. The reason seemed to be that Bill Shand Kydd, apart from being married to his wife's sister, was a responsible businessman and reliable, unlike most of his gambling clique.

It's very strange, aristocrats are different from the common herd. The stereotype of the ruling class with their stoicism in the face of adversity has a basis in fact, even though the origin of the stiff upper lip may have had more to do with concealing bad teeth when only they could afford sweet food. So I wasn't surprised when I went to see the Dowager Countess on Saturday to find her completely in control of her faculties and the situation. I'd been to many households saying 'I'm looking for your husband' or 'I'm looking for your son' and right from the start they fall apart. It wasn't like that with Lucan's mother, no cringing, no wringing of hands, saying 'What a terrible thing. What's happening to my poor John? Where is he? What has he done?' She was very matter-of-fact and down-to-earth. I would have been suspicious if it had been anyone else but not with an aristocrat, they are a strange breed. I liked the aristocracy, with the exception of a few inevitable black sheep, they seldom misbehaved or broke the law and I always found them most courteous and helpful when I had need to speak to them.

The flat of the Dowager Countess on the eighth floor of a block close to Lord's cricket ground was comfortable, well furnished in the chintzy sort of way you would expect of a rich granny. There were lots of books, but it wasn't cluttered up with military memorabilia. Like her husband, the Dowager Countess came from a military background, the only daughter of Captain the Honourable Edward Dawson, Royal Navy. She had taken the title Dowager on the death of her husband and it fitted her well. She had the tough look of those matriarchal women who for generations kept the home fires burning while their menfolk were off killing one another.

I had gone to the flat with Sgt Forsyth so he could take a full statement from her. A woman detective constable, Sally Bower, was to interview Lady Frances about the events of Thursday night. My purpose in going to see the Dowager Countess was not so much to gain fresh information but to get an impression of her. First impressions are important to policemen. Despite her age she was a formidable character. She still had her wits about her and I judged her to be nobody's fool. I think she had a shrewd idea of exactly what was going on and what her son had done. The newspapers had already printed a lot about the hunt for Lucan and I had no doubt she was also being kept well informed by other members of the family and friends. I didn't ask and I didn't expect her to tell me who had been in touch. She said only what she needed to say, and if she hadn't been guarded about her son I would have wondered why. I asked her if she had any idea where he might be, she replied: 'No.'

The two-page statement taken some time later by DC Sally Bower from Lady Frances was excellent. I found Frances to be a highly intelligent ten-year-old. She wasn't at all horror struck by what had happened. Like her grandmother she was taking it in her stride with amazing resilience.

In the relevant part of her statement Frances said:

> On Thursday evening we, that's Mummy, George, Camilla and Sandra and I, all had our tea together. I think that was sometime around 5.00 p.m. or 5.30 p.m. After tea I played with one of my games in the nursery. Then, at about 7.30 p.m., I watched *Top of*

the *Pops* on the television in the nursery. Mummy, Camilla, George and Sandra were downstairs in Mummy's room. They were watching *The Six Million Dollar Man*. I went down and joined them at about 8.05 p.m., and we all watched the television in Mummy's room. When the programme finished at 8.30 p.m. I went back upstairs to the nursery and played a little more with my game. Sandra brought George and Camilla upstairs and put them to bed. I had a bath before I started watching television and was wearing my pyjamas after my bath. I stayed in the nursery for about five minutes only, then I went downstairs again to Mummy's room. That would have been about 8.40 p.m.

I asked Mummy where Sandra was and she said she was downstairs making some tea. I didn't see her go downstairs so I don't know if she took any empty cups with her. I didn't notice whether or not there were any empty cups in the room. After a while Mummy said she wondered why Sandra was so long. I don't know what time this was, but it was before the news came on the television at 9 p.m. I said I would go downstairs to see what was keeping Sandra but Mummy said no, she would go. I said I would go with her but she said no, it was okay, she would go. Mummy left the room to go downstairs and I stayed watching the television. She left the bedroom door open, but there was no light in the hall because the light bulb is worn out and it doesn't work.

Just after Mummy left the room I heard a scream. It sounded as though it came from a long way away. I thought maybe the cat had scratched Mummy and she had screamed. I wasn't frightened by the scream and I just stayed in the room watching television. I went to the door of the room and called out Mummy, but there was no answer so I just left it.

At about 9.05 p.m., when the news was on the television, Daddy and Mummy both walked into the room. Mummy had blood over her face and she was crying. Mummy told me to go upstairs. Daddy didn't say anything to me and I didn't say anything to either of them. I don't know how much blood was on Mummy's face, I only caught a glimpse of her. As far as I can remember, Daddy was wearing a pair of dark trousers and an overcoat which was full length and fawn coloured with brown checks. I was sitting on the bed as they came in the door and I couldn't see them very well. There were two lights on above Mummy's bed and one other sidelight on. I didn't hear any conversation between Mummy and Daddy. I couldn't see if Daddy's clothes had any blood on them. I wondered what had happened but I didn't ask.

After Mummy told me to go upstairs I got straight up and went upstairs to my bedroom, which is on the top floor of the house. I got into bed and read my book. I didn't hear anything from downstairs. After a little while, I don't know how long because I don't have a clock in my room, I heard Daddy calling out for Mummy. He was calling out: 'Veronica, where are you?' I got up and went to the banisters and looked down and I saw Daddy coming out of the nursery on the floor below me. He then went into the bathroom on the same floor as the nursery. He came straight out and then he went downstairs.

That was the last I saw of him. He never came up to the top floor of the house that night, either to look for Mummy or to say goodnight to me. I didn't notice at any time whether or not Daddy was wearing gloves. The last time I saw Sandra was when she took George and Camilla upstairs to bed. I was very surprised to see Daddy at home that Thursday night, but I never asked why he was there.

The statement brought back by the officer who went to see the Maxwell-Scotts at their home at Uckfield, a country house called Grants Hill House, amazed us. Lucan hadn't just driven through Uckfield, he had actually called on his friends and spent some time there. Ian Maxwell-Scott was away in London but his 38-year-old wife Susan was at home when he turned up at about 11.30 p.m. He rang the doorbell and she looked out of the window and saw him standing outside so she invited him in. He looked a little dishevelled, wearing a blue polo-neck shirt, brown sleeveless pullover and grey flannels with a dark patch on the right hip. She gave him a whisky and he telephoned his mother and tried unsuccessfully to call Bill Shand Kydd. Lucan had asked her for some notepaper and had written two letters to Bill Shand Kydd which he asked her to post. They had coffee and talked for a while before he left at about 1.15 a.m., driving off in a dark-coloured car and giving the impression he was going to return to London.

Broadly, the story Lucan had told her as related in her statement was the same as the one he told his mother: that he had seen a man attacking his wife through the blinds of the basement window. He had let himself into the house with his own key and gone down into the basement. What he had seen was horrifying and, after he had slipped in a pool of blood, he saw the man run off. Veronica was in an appalling state with blood all over her and he took her upstairs to her bed and calmed her down because she was in a state of hysteria, shouting that he had paid the man to murder her. After he went to the bathroom to get some clean towels to clean her up he returned to the bedroom and found she had gone. He was in the house with blood on him and, knowing Veronica would try and incriminate him, he panicked and left the house to get away from it all. It was, he told her, an unbelievable nightmare experience.

The tale of the mystery intruder was obviously going to be the basis of Lucan's defence when we caught up with him and stood him up in court on a murder charge. It wasn't that which bothered us when we read Susan Maxwell-Scott's statement, it was her actions after Lucan called at her house. The letters written by Lucan to Bill Shand Kydd had been posted by her children on Friday and she was the last person as far as we knew to see him alive. She was a qualified barrister so was evidently not a stupid woman, yet she had not seen fit to contact the police despite the fact every newspaper and every TV and radio broadcast said we were scouring the country for him. According to her statement, Lucan had been with her for nearly two hours, so there must have been a lot more said than was included in her statement. I very much wanted to speak to her myself. Why, among other things, did she think he would be writing letters if he was going back to London to clear everything up?

6 The Hand that Rocked the Cradle

The high society wedding of Lucan and Veronica took place on 28 November 1963. Veronica, an attractive 26-year-old with blue eyes and long blonde hair, looked stunning in a silk gown, her tulle veil held in place by an expensive diamond tiara 'borrowed' from the Dowager Countess. The ceremony at Holy Trinity Church, Brompton, was followed by a lavish champagne reception at the Carlton Tower Hotel. On the face of it the couple looked well suited, but behind his back Lucan's friends said the marriage was a mistake and rightly predicted that it wouldn't last. They felt the couple were a mismatch because Veronica was a commoner with a middle-class upbringing and stuffy Lucan would have been better wed to a society deb who might more easily tolerate his frailties.

By the standards of most people Veronica herself would be considered to have had a good start in life, with private schooling and a pony to ride. She was born the daughter of First World War One major Charles Moorehouse Duncan. He was killed in a car crash in 1939 when she was only two, leaving his 21-year-old wife Thelma a widow and pregnant with Veronica's younger sister Christina. Her mother took her daughters to live in Bournemouth and, when Veronica was ten, they went to South Africa where Thelma married James Margrie, who had been an RAF navigator in the war and held prisoner by the Germans. They returned to England where Jim took the tenancy of the Wheatsheaf Hotel, a Hampshire country pub at North Waltham near Basingstoke. The girls went to St Swithin's school at Winchester but Veronica disliked it and was happy to leave at seventeen to spend a year attending an art college in Bournemouth. She moved to London, intent on a career modelling, but at 5 ft 2 in she was too small for the fashion catwalks and gave up the idea after a poorly paid stint as a house model for a clothing firm. Secretarial temping work followed and running a little printing business with some friends. She shared a flat in Melbury Road, Kensington, with her sister Christina and three other girl friends. When Christina met and married Bill Shand Kydd it was to transform their lives.

Veronica fell in love with Lucan shortly after Christina's marriage. On 17 January 1963 she was chief bridesmaid at the wedding, in the same church where she was to take her vows with Lucan only ten months later. At the country home of the Shand Kydd family at Leighton Buzzard in Bedfordshire she was introduced to Lucan at a drinks party after a golf match. In August Lucan was again invited as a weekend guest at Horton Hall and he asked Bill Shand Kydd if Veronica could be there. The marriage proposal followed a whirlwind romance, Lucan buying a ring from Cartier to seal their engagement. Veronica was so deeply in love with the dashing Lucan she failed to appreciate the inherent dangers in his precarious vocation as a full-time gambler. Veronica had always lived in the shadow of her taller and more exuberant sister Christina, but marriage into the aristocracy would put them on level terms.

The honeymoon travelling on the Orient Express to Istanbul was the start of an idyllic period in her life with the man she adored. When, in the early hours of the morning of 21 January 1964 Lucan's father died at his home in London at the age of sixty-five, her husband suddenly became the 7th Earl of Lucan. In the space of only two months Veronica had changed from being plain Miss Duncan to Lady Lucan. Along with the colourful bag of titles from his family heritage Lucan received an inheritance worth an estimated £250,000, a tidy fortune when the average wage was only £16 a week. It enabled the newlyweds to buy the lease of 46 Lower Belgrave Street for £19,000 in July 1964 and to indulge in entertaining and world travel on a lavish scale. Only a month after the death of his father Lucan flew to America to be at the ringside when Muhammad Ali, then Cassius Clay, knocked out Sonny Liston for the world heavyweight title. Veronica's photo album was to become filled with pictures taken in the pleasure grounds of Europe and America. The photo album itself was soon to play a part in the death of one of Lucan's closest friends, Dominic Elwes, as the ripples from the murder spread.

Wherever he went the suave Lucan was to be found at the

gaming tables in the nearest casino, emulating the tuxedoed Sean Connery in the James Bond movies. The thought obviously crossed the mind of film producer Cubby Broccoli, for when Connery retired from the role he considered the square-jawed Lucan as his replacement as 007. I was told that, in one of those odd coincidences, the man who got the part to play Bond in the film *On Her Majesty's Secret Service*, George Lazenby, was a previous tenant of Lucan's flat in Elizabeth Street. Lucan was also tested by Italian director Vittorio de Sica for the 1967 film *Woman Times Seven* to play a gambling English lord opposite Shirley MacLaine in one of the sketches that was to feature the likes of Peter Sellers and Michael Caine. It was a role that would have suited him down to the ground, but in his screen tests he came over as too stiff in front of the cameras. By another coincidence Vittorio de Sica died less than a week after Lucan vanished.

Nannies are respected members of top drawer households, well looked after in retirement, sometimes passing the position on to their daughters to provide a continuity of devoted service. They have strictly defined roles, are usually trained at establishments like the Norland College or the Chiltern Nursery Training College. They are what the public expect a nanny working for the gentry to be when they see them pushing old-fashioned prams like Mary Poppins in posh London parks, prim in starched uniforms and round hats. Sandra Rivett wasn't a Norlander, nor did she hold a National Nursery Examination Board Diploma. She had no qualifications as a nanny and was more akin to being an *au pair*. In addition to looking after the Lucan's three children she performed tasks which a traditional Scottish nanny would never deign to do, undertaking household chores, carrying out errands and generally acting as a companion to the lonely and isolated Veronica. There had been a succession of nannies, eight in less than two years, some staying only a very short time. They left for a variety of reasons, but Lucan insisted it was because of the unreasonable behaviour of his wife. Sandra had only been the nanny for a few weeks, since 26 August, having secured the position through an agency. Only hours before her death she talked to her mother, Mrs Eunice Hensby, on the telephone, telling her she was happy in the job and enjoyed looking after the children and making plans to visit her parents at Christmas. Sandra got on well with Veronica despite, or perhaps because of, her working-class background, and she was loved by the children. Tragically, she was to be in the wrong place at the wrong time.

At the age of twenty-nine Sandra was a product of the fun-loving 1960s with its liberal morals. She had left secondary modern school at Caterham in Surrey and was employed as an apprentice hairdresser and in a factory before working as a nanny for a doctor at Croydon and as a nurse in an old people's home. In 1967 she married Roger Rivett, a sailor in the Royal Navy, but they finally split up in May 1974 after several trial separations. Sandra had a young son of her own when she was nineteen who was adopted by her parents soon after he was born. At the time of her death, he believed Sandra to be his elder sister. Red-headed and vivacious, Sandra loved going to dances with a girlfriend and was attractive to the men she met. She was receptive to their advances and there were a lot of boyfriends in the little address book and diary I took from her room in my search of the Lucan house.

While Veronica had told us Lucan had attacked her and apparently had killed Sandra, we only had her word for it. We were aware a defence lawyer might seek to prove Sandra was the intended victim, deliberately murdered in a crime of passion, either by her ex-husband, a jealous lover or even Lucan himself. Her character could be viciously attacked so we had to prove beyond any shadow of a doubt the assailant was Lucan and Veronica, not Sandra, was the woman he planned to kill. Sandra's husband, who was working then at Gatwick Airport as a security guard, was soon eliminated from enquiries. He was with his girlfriend and her family at the time. Her current boyfriend, a 26-year-old Australian barman named John Hankins who she had met at the Plumbers Arms, was also quickly ruled out. He had spoken to her on the phone that night but was working as a relief barman in the Kings Arms public house at Shepherds Market when the killer struck the fatal blows. Everyone who was in her address book was seen and we were entirely satisfied nobody intended her harm and that she was an innocent casualty of the war going on between the Lucans.

What we did establish was that Thursday was normally Sandra's day off. Lady Frances told us the children had spent the previous weekend away with their father. Her sister Camilla had informed him Sandra had boyfriends and went out with them. Lucan had asked when this was and Camilla said it was on her days off. Lucan had then asked Frances what day Sandra was off and she had said Thursdays. That was critical. Lucan knew what day Sandra would be out, but he did not know she had swopped it that week. What he also believed was that on days when the nanny was off, Frances did not go to school, maintaining to friends it was because Veronica was too lazy to take her. On the day of the murder he rang the Glendower School which Frances attended and asked headmistress Marguerite Jackson if she was there, thinking if she wasn't it would confirm Sandra was off for the day. Mrs Jackson said she did not know and would find out, but when she twice rang back Lucan did not answer. Had he been told Frances was not at school it would only have strengthened his belief that Veronica would be on her own that night. She would go down to the basement kitchen to get a drink and a sandwich and he would be waiting to strike. He was not to know that Sandra was at home. Ironically, Frances said in her statement she did not go to school that day because the bus did not come for her. The scene was set. Sandra would carry the tray of dirty crockery down into the darkness of the basement and meet her death.

We needed to test Lucan's story to his mother that he had been passing No. 46 and had looked in through the basement window and seen an intruder fighting with Veronica. We didn't believe it for one minute, but it was necessary to show to anyone raising it at a later stage that we had put it to the test. On Saturday, 9 November, at 10 p.m., roughly the same time of night that the attacks had taken place, I carried out a series of experiments with Roy Ranson and Detective Inspector Charlie Hulls. Driving past the house it was not possible to see the basement window because of cars parked in the street. We tried it driving each way because we didn't know which direction Lucan was supposed to be going. He might even be saying he was walking by so we tried that as well. Standing on the pavement, with the lights in the basement and breakfast room switched on, it was difficult to see in through the venetian blinds even when they were open. Only by kneeling down with my head about two feet from the pavement was it possible to see through the kitchen part of the basement into the breakfast room and make out two or three steps of the stairs leading up. Even the most credulous of juries would scarcely believe Lucan had by chance found himself kneeling down on the pavement peering into the window.

If, as Veronica claimed, she was attacked at the top of the stairs in the hallway it would be impossible to see anywhere near that far up, even lying flat out on the ground. The forensic evidence supported her story: there was her blood on the carpet in the ground floor passage leading to the stairs and on the walls. If Lucan was telling the truth he would have needed x-ray eyes like the *Six Million Dollar Man* to see through the brick walls of the house. There was also the trifling matter of how the intruder got into the house in the first place. As the door hadn't been forced he could only have entered by using a key. He must have moved like greased lightning, too, to have got the body into the mail-bag in the short space of time it would have taken for Lucan to have reached the scene after seeing the attack taking place.

At 2.40 p.m. on Sunday, 10 November, Detective Sgt David DeLima, of the Sussex Constabulary, found Michael Stoop's Ford Corsair at Newhaven. It was among parked cars in Norman Road, a back street of terraced houses. He told his station and they informed the murder squad as he kept observation on the blue saloon. Roy Ranson went to the scene, together with Detective Inspector Charlie Hulls, DC Bob Morgan, the exhibits officer, and a local detective inspector.

The boot of the car was locked and Roy Ranson's driver, PC Alec Neil, forced it open. Inside, lying on top of old clothing and papers, was a piece of lead piping, bound in medical tape and to all intents and purposes similar to that found at the murder scene. The only difference was that the tape wrapped around this pipe was white, whereas that used to club Sandra Rivett to death and batter Veronica Lucan was blood-stained, squashed and bent with the force of the impacts. Everything in the car was photographed and it was put on a trailer and taken to the Metropolitan Police laboratory at Lambeth for forensic investigation. Blood found with hair on the floor of the car by the driver's foot pedals was identified as similar to that of both the women who had been attacked. A smear along the window on the driver's side was Group B – Sandra Rivett's – and that on the dashboard was the more common Group A – Veronica's. There was also blood on both front seats, on the map box between them and on the steering wheel.

Contrary to what people believe from fictionalized film and TV shows, cars don't make good subjects for fingerprint experts to examine. They have laminated surfaces and marks are hard to pick up from the steering wheel as they are smudged by the continual movement of hands. A partial print that could have been Lucan's was lifted off the rear-view mirror, matching up with one found at his flat. Apart from blood stains the car revealed very little, except that fibres matching those on the murder weapon were found on material in the boot. What was important about the car was that it was discovered at Newhaven, a small coastal port on the Sussex coast. The port has a ferry plying regularly across the channel to Dieppe in France and is used by small freighters, either going to or from mainland Europe or around the coast. What was interesting was that Norman Road was on the other side of the river to the ferry port, nearer the berths of the fishing fleet and the marina with its many yachts and speedboats.

Immediately after the car was found it was agreed that Sussex police would carry out the house-to-house inquiries to see if anyone had seen it arrive, concentrating on the area 50 yards each side of its parking place in Norman Road. They found a witness living nearby who was being treated for bad eyes. He was advised by his doctor to look out the window when he got up at night and focus his eyes on some object. He would look at a neighbour's car, and he said when he looked out at 4 a.m. on Friday morning it wasn't there for some reason, but when he looked out again at 8 a.m. the gap was filled by the Ford Corsair. Obviously the car had arrived some time after 4 a.m., but where had it been after it left Susan Maxwell-Scott's? She said Lucan drove off at 1.15 a.m. and the short journey from Uckfield to Newhaven would take under half-an-hour at that time of night. Even if the car was dumped right after 4 a.m., and allowing for her giving only an approximate time, there was still a missing two hours.

Nothing was turned up by Sussex police when they looked at their records of accidents and road checks carried out in the area that night. Extensive inquiries were also carried out to determine if anyone in Newhaven had seen someone answering the description of Lucan. There wasn't a lot of industry in the town so many people would be travelling to work on Friday morning to London, Brighton, Eastbourne or Seaford. It was a daily routine. If they didn't drive they would use the same bus each day or the same train, usually sitting in exactly the same seats. Ferry terminal and rail station staff were questioned, together with bus conductors and their passengers. Nobody saw a stranger, particularly a tall man as striking as Lucan. He was well capable of escaping by boat, but there were no reports of any missing from the river or the marina. If Lucan had been in Newhaven it was difficult to see how he left the town without someone seeing him. The car he was driving that night was certainly in Newhaven and there was no doubt somebody had taken it there, but was it Lucan? We had found the cart, but where was the horse?

7　The Upstairs, Downstairs Murder

The golden age for the Lucans lasted for several years and it was difficult to pinpoint the exact turning point when their marriage began heading for the rocks. Lady Frances was born in October, 1964, and Veronica was probably disappointed at not providing an immediate heir to the title with their first child. Lord George came along to rectify the situation in the autumn of 1967, after which Veronica suffered from post-natal depression. She went through a difficult pregnancy with their third child, Lady Camilla, born in 1970, but by then the marriage was already in deep trouble because of Lucan's obsessive gambling.

For reasons that were difficult to understand Veronica had gone night after night to the Clermont Club where Lucan would indulge his passion for gambling. While he either lost or won large sums of money into the early hours she would sit alone watching television. Unlike Lucan's other clubs, the St James and the White's, women were permitted into the sanctity of the Clermont, but it was still an unwelcoming male domain. There were other Clermont wives who sat at what their menfolk called the 'Widows' Table', but none stayed the course as long as Veronica. She said she didn't mind her husband's excessive gambling but she couldn't have enjoyed seeing him go through the tense nightly agony and ecstasy. He had trained his face not to reveal the slightest emotion whatever cards he was dealt, but she had a wife's innate sensitivity to the swings in his fortunes. She could surely not have accompanied him because she was worried he might be unfaithful, though he was attractive to other women. Lucan was totally consumed by his gambling and wasn't at all interested in other women, a man's man in a clubby world where even the sex act itself was looked on as bestowing a favour. They even had a word for it which was adopted with amusement by some of the more chauvinistic members of the murder squad,

The Upstairs, Downstairs Murder 63

'boffing', which apparently derived from the French term *boff de politesse*.

Being a professional gambler was a bizarre occupation in itself, made worse by Veronica's accompanying him to the 'office' to watch him pit his wits against some of the toughest players for high stakes on the circuit. It was inevitable the situation would result in an increasing strain on the marriage. Lucan became convinced his wife was suffering from a psychiatric condition and twice he tried to have her admitted for treatment at private nursing homes, but she refused. She did, however, see psychiatrists and took drugs for depression and anxiety, the side-effects not helping her state of mind. Lucan told friends she was going increasingly insane and he bored them with tales of her odd behaviour in support of his claims. Certainly they could see for themselves that Veronica was a tense woman and there was something odd about constantly following her husband, invading his space. She would keep to herself at the clubs, ignored by Lucan even at the dinner table and not talking to his friends. It was hardly surprising they were prepared to believe his stories about her mental state.

I met Veronica on many occasions and, while she was undoubtedly highly strung and not the sort of person people would easily warm to socially, I did not think she was unbalanced at that time. Certainly she would have been better off creating a life of her own. Veronica's views and opinions were not those shared by Lucan's close circle of chums. In their eyes Lucan was a splendid fellow who could do no wrong, Veronica a shrew who could do nothing right. If she was invited to weekend parties she would be frozen out and would often prefer to take refuge in her room, alone and miserable.

The growing strain on the marriage finally resulted in Lucan leaving No. 46 Lower Belgrave Street on 7 January 1973 and moving later into the furnished flat at 72a Elizabeth Street. The breakup was the start of an increasingly bitter dispute between the unhappy couple over custody of the children. Lucan was convinced his wife was unfit to look after them, setting out to prove Veronica was mistreating them, hiring private detectives to watch and follow her. He was delighted when on 23 March the High Court granted him temporary custody until a full hearing could be held. The same afternoon Lucan and two private detectives picked up George and Camilla from their nanny, Stefanja Sawicka, as she was walking with them in Grosvenor Place on the way home from a stroll in Green Park. Frances was collected when she left school and taken to join George and Camilla at Lucan's flat. The children remained there, being looked after by a different nanny, Jordanka Kotlarova, a Yugoslavian girl, until June when the High Court reversed the earlier ruling and he was ordered to hand them back. Veronica was granted custody of the children after an acrimonious hearing in which they both made virulent accusations against one another. The judge was seemingly more impressed by Veronica's version of events, presumably not happy with Lucan's lifestyle and evidence corroborated by a nanny that he had occasionally knocked her about. Taking the law into his own hands and snatching the children was certainly a major tactical error, a move hardly likely to impress any judge. Dismayed, Lucan was granted what was regarded as reasonable access to the children, able to see them at weekends and school holidays. He had been certain the judge would be sympathetic to him and grant him custody, and when he failed to convince him of his suitability he was devastated. He became obsessed about the children and eventually a desperate measure was to form in his mind.

I was away on leave during the week after the murder, a previously-arranged trip to Majorca. I offered to cancel it, but Roy Ranson said it would not be necessary. We both felt on that first weekend it would only be a short period of time before Lucan was arrested. I was sure when I came back from the sunshine I would find Lucan had surrendered and was in custody. At the very least I thought we would have located him somewhere. It wasn't to be. Not only was there still no sign of the evasive earl, but we were deep in the mire after ten days and digging ourselves further into it. I spent two days ploughing through the statements that had been taken, messages that had come in on the telephone and telex, correspondence and the various actions that had been taken. There was nothing in any of the information to suggest we were any closer to finding Lucan than when I went away. I had a discussion with Roy Ranson and it was clear to both of us we had to reassess the situation.

There were a number of possibilities as to the fate of Lucan: he had killed himself; he had escaped abroad; he had gone into

1 Examining some of the evidence with Roy Ranson – including more than 1,000 statements which were taken

2 Lord Lucan's mother, the Dowager Countess, and his brother-in-law William Shand Kydd in good spirits during the inquest

3 Lord Lucan and his bride Veronica after their wedding in November 1963

Evening Standard

London: Friday November 8 1974

...dy in sack... Countess runs out screaming

BELGRAVIA MURDER —EARL SOUGHT

By JOHN STEVENS, ROBERT McGOWAN, ROGER BRAY and JOHN PONDER

THE 39-year-old Earl of Lucan was still missing this afternoon more than 17 hours after his children's nannie was found savagely murdered at the earl's Belgravia house.

A Scotland Yard spokesman said: "We want to interview Lord Lucan to tell him about the incident. We do not, at the moment, wish to see anybody else."

The nannie was discovered in a sack in the basement. She had been beaten to death, probably with a piece of lead piping.

She was found after 35-year-old Lady Lucan, who had also been battered about the head, ran from the house in Belgrave Street shouting "Murder... murder... murder."

Shortly after the grim discovery, police broke into another house owned by the earl in nearby Eaton Row. He was not there.

Last contact with Lord Lucan was believed to be a telephone call to his mother at her London home at midnight—sometime after the murder.

Today the Dowager Countess said: "I do not want to make any comment."

Lady Lucan was taken to St George's Hospital and her condition was said to be serious. The nannie was named as Sandra Rivett, who lived at Coulsdon, Surrey. Her husband, Roger, went to Gerald Road police station with his mother. He told detectives that he and his wife had been separated for some time.

The attack on Lady Lucan and the nannie was seen by Lady Lucan's 10-year-old daughter Frances.

When battered Lady Lucan got out of the house she staggered to the nearby Plumbers Arms for help.

Head barman Derrick Whitehouse, 44, described the scene: "She was suffering from various head wounds. They were quite severe," he said. "She was covered in blood and was bleeding profusely. She was just in a delirious state and

Contd. Back Page, Col. 3

LORD LUCAN

LADY LUCAN—in hospital with serious head injuries

● The man they call Lucky Lucan — News on camera : Page Three

INSIDE YOUR STANDARD

Second man dies, three lose legs in pub blast
Page 6

Milhench jailed for Wilson forgery
Page 5

The last day in Covent Garden
Page 11

Londoner's Diary Page 18
Recipe Page 22
Motoring News Page 40
TV and radio Page 2

Spending cuts 'will hit schools'
Page 15

Emergency plan to halt famine
Page 16

Entertainment - - 20

THE NEW MUSTANG II

SIMPSONS OF WEMBLEY

4 The first of many newspaper headlines which appeared on the day after Sandra Rivett's death as the high society murder became big news

5 Hotel proprietress Suzanne Guilpain *centre* claimed Lord Lucan stayed at The Grand in Cherbourg. She describes him to Roy Ranson and me through interpreter Glynne Rhys-Evans

6 Susan Maxwell-Scott and her husband Ian whose house at Uckfield Lord Lucan visited after the murder

7 Sandra Rivett, the nanny brutally beaten to death at 46 Lower Belgrave Street

8 Talking to a diver probing the harbour at Newhaven for Lord Lucan's body as part of a widespread search of the south coast

9   With the press corps at a seafront bar in St Malo. On the left are Jon Snow, Peter Birkett and Michael Fielder while Owen Summers and John Penrose are on the right with Roy Ranson and Glynne Rhys-Evans

10 With then Prime Minister Harold Wilson who had invited us to his retirement party at 10 Downing Street to thank us for recovering his stolen tax papers. *Left to right:* me, my wife Pat, Harold Wilson, Irene Ranson and Roy Ranson

"This bit 'all the best David' signed LL check it for fingerprints!"

11 A cartoon by Wren which appeared on my retirement from the Metropolitan Police

12 John Aspinall rubs his jaw after being punched for what he said at the memorial service for Lord Lucan's friend Dominic Elwes

hiding alone; or somebody was sheltering him. Whatever the answer the trail was getting cold. When that happens in a murder inquiry it is difficult to artificially warm it up again. We needed to broaden the scope of the inquiry. It was decided I would spend the following week in Newhaven, the last known plot on the map we had of Lucan because that was where the car he was driving was found. It was reasonable to suppose Newhaven was where he had been, if indeed it was Lucan who dumped the car and it wasn't left there by somebody else as a red herring. A search had already been carried out at Newhaven but it was felt a more detailed one might throw up something new. In the meantime it was agreed I would return to No. 46 and his flat and go over them with a fine tooth comb to see if there was anything we had missed that might give us a lead.

While I was away Roy Ranson had been to Bow Street magistrates court to apply for warrants for the arrest of Lucan. They were granted by magistrate Mr Evelyn Russell after a short hearing before the court sat for its scheduled cases. There were two warrants, one accusing Lucan of the murder of Sandra Rivett, the other for the attempted murder of Veronica. Lucan was still front page news. On the Tuesday the warrants were issued the *Evening Standard* printed the headline WANTED FOR MURDER alongside his photograph. Roy Ranson was quoted in the *Daily Telegraph* the next day saying: 'The necessary messages have been sent to police forces throughout the world who are looking for him and they will detain him on my behalf if they can find him. I am now in a position to have him arrested abroad. I have sufficient evidence to take the action I have taken. He may be anywhere and I have to cover all of this. I do not know whether he is abroad or in this country, but he has friends in many foreign countries and there are also addresses in America. They are being checked by the local police.' Asked if he thought somebody might be hiding Lucan he said: 'Anybody who is now harbouring, aiding or abetting him will be arrested for the offence of harbouring a wanted man.'

The evening after the warrants were issued Bill Shand Kydd went on prime time television on ITV, the commercial channel, and appealed for Lucan to give himself up. He was asked by the interviewer on *News at Ten* what message he had for Lucan if he was watching. He replied: 'I'd say, get hold of me, or David Leverton [a solicitor] as soon as possible, and we'll go to the police station.' There had been no response from Lucan. In the *Daily Mail* the following morning Susan Maxwell-Scott was quoted as saying she was 'amazed and aghast' that arrest warrants had been issued, adding: 'He has to be innocent.'

The media were still taking a huge interest in the case. It was inevitably dubbed the 'Upstairs, Downstairs' murder because of the popular London Weekend TV series that had been running since 1970. The programme followed the fortunes of Lord Bellamy and his family after the turn of the century, and James, a cad who was not above borrowing money from the servants, bore a remarkable resemblance to the moustachiod Lucan.

Fleet Street's finest set up their detached headquarters in a pub we used in Belgravia officially called The Duke of Wellington but affectionately know as The Duke of Boots. It was a convivial hostelry run by tenant licensee Joe Mercer and his wife Agnes with the help of their son John and a manager named George who was a character in his own right. The pub was popular with young Belgravia blades and Joe kept a glass on a shelf behind the bar stuffed full of their bounced cheques. Joe rarely complained to the police and somehow the debts would get paid.

For the press corps and the murder squad 'The Boots' provided an ideal venue to exchange news and gossip. Newspapers are plugged into a huge international network with vast research sources so we were able to gain access to this. We were also able to feed journalists both news we wanted them to print to assist in the hunt and background information to point them in the right direction. I already knew most of the crime reporters from previous cases. They were old trusted friends, so these informal get-togethers were important to all of us.

Another important development while I was away was the arrival of a third letter, apparently written by Lucan after the murder. It was sent to Michael Stoop at the St James Club and was delivered by a postman at 9.15 a.m. on Monday 11 November. Frank Read, the head receptionist at the club, said the letter was unstamped so he had to pay an excess charge of seven pence for it. He had given the letter to Michael Stoop who had handed it on to the murder squad the following day. Unfortunately he didn't notice where the envelope was postmarked and had thrown it away. Despite an intensive search of the waste bins at the club, the envelope hadn't been found.

The letter was written on the blotting paper from a pad of Lion Brand writing paper which Michael Stoop said was in the cubbyhole of the car Lucan had borrowed. It was matched up with a pad found by the scenes of crimes officer who examined the car. The letter said:

Dear Michael
    I have had a traumatic night of unbelievable coincidences. However, I won't bore you with anything or involve you except to say that when you come across my children, which I hope you will, please tell them that you knew me and that all I cared about was them.
    The fact that a crooked solicitor and a rotten psychiatrist destroyed me between them will be of no importance to the children.
    I gave Bill Shand Kydd an account of what actually happened but judging by my last effort in court, no-one, let alone a 67-year-old judge, would believe – and I no longer care except that my children should be protected.
Yours ever
John

Again, the letter was carefully scrutinized, its content analysed. The reference to a 'crooked solicitor' and 'rotten psychiatrist' were taken to be something to do with the High Court action over custody of the children. In this letter Lucan had given the impression he was not likely ever to see his children again, suggesting he was about to commit suicide. It could have been deliberate, to put off his pursuers. The opening paragraph about a night of 'unbelievable coincidences' might have been phrased with a similar ulterior motive, to suggest he was innocent. There could be similar reasoning behind the paragraph saying he had told Bill Shand Kydd what actually happened – interrupting a fight in the basement. Taken together, the two letters formed the basis of a defence. It was an achievement of remarkable clarity for a man who knew nothing of the law and was fleeing in panic. What the letters to Bill Shand Kydd and Michael Stoop did not look like were suicide notes. In my experience suicide notes invariably start off: 'When you read this I will be dead.' People about to kill themselves do not sit down and calmly write cleverly phrased letters like these.

* * *

Belgravia, taking its name from the Grosvenor estate at Belgrave in Cheshire, is based on four squares: Belgrave, Eaton, Lowndes and Chester, laid out by builder Thomas Cubitt on what were previously hayfields and joined by a network of terraces and roads. Chester Square lies between Lower Belgrave Street and Elizabeth Street and it was here we were to find a woman who thought she spoke on the telephone to Lucan on the night of the murder. This wasn't picked up in the house-to-house enquiries but came to our attention some days later. Mrs Madelaine Florman noticed two red spots on her stone doorstep some days after the murder and spoke about them to a friend of Lucan's, Dominic Elwes. He mentioned it in an interview with the police and swab samples were taken off the white stone. They turned out to be blood, so it basically confirmed the story the woman told us about the happenings on the night.

Mrs Florman said she was in bed when she was woken up by the ringing of the front door bell at what she thought was about 10.30 p.m. Her husband was out at the time so she did not answer it, thinking it might be passing youths playing games. She went back to sleep and was later woken up by the ringing of her bedside telephone. She picked up the receiver and a man said: 'Madelaine?' She replied: 'Yes.' The man said: 'I know you ...', and his voice then disintegrated into an incoherent jumble of words. These didn't make any sense so she put down the receiver.

There was a connection in that Mrs Florman's daughter went to the same school as Frances and she thought the caller could have been Lucan. We deduced he may have been ringing her doorbell to ask her to go to No. 46 to look after his children, knowing they were alone in the house after Veronica had run out. Forensic examination of the blood stains showed they came from Group B, the same as Sandra Rivett. Unfortunately Mrs Florman was unable to pinpoint at what time the caller rang on the telephone, so we were unable to determine where he might have made the call. All the telephone boxes in the area were checked for blood stains but none were found. Neither did we know how Lucan had got to her doorstep, either on foot or, more likely, driving Michael Stoop's car, stepping out and leaving the blood stain on the step.

He could then have taken two routes out of London to

Uckfield, either over Vauxhall Bridge and down the A23 and A22 through East Grinstead, or down the Old Kent Road and the A21 via Tunbridge Wells. It was my guess he crossed Vauxhall Bridge and drove down through Streatham to Croydon, a route he would know to the South Coast and would follow unconsciously in his terror. He would be expecting any moment for a police patrol car with flashing lights to stop him. When that didn't happen and he got out into the countryside he relaxed, took stock of where he was, and decided to continue on the 44-mile journey to the Maxwell-Scott house at Uckfield.

8 Last Throw of the Dice

After he lost the High Court case for custody of his children Lucan went into a marked decline. Friends noticed a disturbing change in his personality. His intake of neat vodka increased and he chain-smoked, his normally equitable temperament replaced by morose moods and occasional temper tantrums. His depression affected his play, a settled homelife being an essential requisite for the concentration needed by a gambler to calculate odds and make essential judgements on opposing players. Brooding on the unfairness of the court decision and how to prove to the world the insanity of Veronica was not conducive to being a winner. He lost his confidence and magician's touch. He spoke to his friends incessantly about bugging devices to tape damning conversations with her, leading them to believe he had acquired a miniature tape recorder to conceal about his person for the purpose. If he did have one, we never found it among his possessions. All we found at his flat was a normal recorder and a number of standard cassette tapes.

I listened to all of the tapes, which were merely recordings of telephone conversations he had had with Veronica. They were pathetic rather than revealing. He had not goaded her into making injudicious remarks as was suggested, nor had she said anything that would be of the slightest use to him as a pointer to any mental illness. The conversations were totally banal: 'Hello' ... 'How are you?' ... 'What have you been doing?' and so on, punctuated by torturous long pauses. They were not recordings Lucan could ever produce as evidence, nor were they something that were of any value to us. The impression I gathered was that Lucan was himself disturbed, his head full of the psycho-babble he read in the solitude of his flat as he sought to get evidence to show Veronica was losing her marbles. The 'dreams of paranoia' phrase he used in his letter to Bill Shand Kydd might have meant something to a psychiatrist, but it meant nothing to me.

Lucan had other pressing matters on his mind, too: mounting financial problems. In 1972 his friend John Aspinall had sold the Clermont to Playboy, a Chicago-based organization built up by Hugh Hefner on the profits of his girlie magazine and expanding into hotels and casinos. It wasn't only the fact Playboy used 'bunny girls' as croupiers that was viewed by Lucan with repulsion. The whole ethos of the American empire as epitomized by Playboy he regarded as vulgar and lacking in taste. For perennial playboys like Old Etonian Dai Llewellyn, Playboy provided a steady supply of playmates, but Lucan was not interested in the Bunnies. Dai, son of Sir Harry 'Foxhunter' Llewellyn, worked for a while at the Clermont as a public relations officer, as did Latin lovely Viviane Ventura.

The opening of the first Playboy Club in Europe in London's Park Lane had come just after gambling had been legalized on 29 July 1960. The Betting and Gaming Act was known as the 'Vicars Charter' because the intention was to legalize minor gambling like whist drives in church halls. But it was easy for smart entrepeneurs to exploit loopholes and casinos sprung up all over the country, more than a thousand in the next decade. At least with casinos legalized it put a stop to many of the crooked games being run by gangsters, but not all the new arrivals on the gambling scene were regarded as totally honest either. Legitimate businessmen saw the potential as well and, after Crockford's opened in 1961, John Aspinall responded by opening the opulent Clermont at 44 Berkeley Square the following year. Playboy profited from the change in the new law, too, and finally bought the lease of the Clermont from John Aspinall for something over £500,000. The fun days in the early 1960s when 'Aspers' would host lavish parties were long gone, the aristocracy crippled by inheritance taxes, now replaced by would-be playboys in pursuit of the American dream as promoted in the titillating centrefold of *Playboy* magazine.

Some of the surviving upper class crowd who had previously formed the nucleus of the Clermont clientele took the same view as Lucan and departed, their places filled by oil-rich Arabs who would think nothing of betting in sums that would make even Lucan blink. Worse still, Middle Eastern royalty was not so overawed at mixing with a genuine British Lord as celebrity-impressed Americans, so his value to the club as good furniture was that much diminished. With John Aspinall at the helm Lucan had enjoyed a comfortable lifestyle as a house player, not an employee as such, but making up the numbers at high stakes chemmy games to keep outside punters betting. Even after Playboy took over he remained on the list for free drink and the club's excellent food in return for adding class and sophistication, but he was not so involved as a gambler. Aspinall also had an ambivalent attitude towards gambling debts, knowing his players would eventually settle up as a matter of honour. Extrovert Playboy executive Victor Lownes was more hard-nosed about money when he wasn't partying at Stocks, his mansion in Hertfordshire. Without John Aspinall's protection Lucan was in deep trouble, unable to resurrect the confidence and sure gambling instinct that had once made him a legendary winner. He kept up the appearance of a devil-may-care gambler, but it was a sham. He was forced by lack of funds to cut down on the time he could spend sitting in his regular chair playing backgammon.

Like many a gambler before him, Lucan had discovered luck has a nasty habit of looking the other way just when it is needed most. His winning touch had deserted him. What had made the situation considerably worse was the ruinous custody case which resulted in a legal bill of some £40,000 built up over the year-long battle, plus another £4,000 in court costs. In short, he was penniless and needed to raise the wind. He arranged for some family silver to be sold at auction through Christie's, something his ancestors had managed to avoid despite their own financial troubles. But even that would only pay off part of the total debts owning. Something more drastic was required, a master stroke to settle all the debts so he could resume his infatuation for gambling. An idea formed in his mind, either as a blinding flash or gradually creeping into his consciousness over a period of time. It occurred to him that if Veronica was simply to disappear all his problems would vanish with her. He would be able to sell the lease on either 46 Lower Belgrave Street or 5 Eaton Row to raise well over £50,000 which, with the sale of the silver, would put him back in credit. He would also be able to give up the flat that was costing £600 a quarter and, better still, he would have total possession of what mattered to him most, his children. But how to make Veronica disappear? If the idea of killing her at first appeared too fanciful and scarey, it made compelling sense the more he thought about it. Like a bobsleigh hurtling down the ice of the Cresta run on the wrong line, he was out of control and heading for disaster.

The address books removed from Lucan's flat revealed hundreds of names, each of which had to be checked out. It seemed just about everyone interesting he ever met he jotted down. The vast majority of those questioned barely knew him at all or hadn't seen him for a long time. Typical was Mrs Brady Tucker in America who told the New York police that Lucan hadn't been in touch with her for years. It took a lot of sorting out, but in the end we were able to discount most of the names and come up with a shortlist of Lucan's relatives and most intimate friends, people who were being dubbed the Lucan Set. In one way or another they would all be involved in our enquiries. This was the list, in alphabetical order:

JOHN ASPINALL. 'Aspers' to his friends. Opened the Clermont in 1962 after running floating chemmy games. A close friend of Lucan.

MICHAEL HICKS BEACH. Old Etonian. Literary agent.

CHARLES BENSON. Old Etonian. Racing correspondent of the *Daily Express*, known as 'The Scout'. He played golf regularly with Lucan and Ian Maxwell-Scott.

THE HON. HUGH BINGHAM. Younger brother of Lucan. Not a gambler, a mineral prospector.

MARK BIRLEY. Old Etonian. Opened Annabel's, the world's best-known disco, in the basement of the Clermont, naming it after his wife, Lady Annabel, who had become Goldsmith's mistress.

ANDRINA COLQUHOUN. Photographer and ex-debutante. Step-daughter of timber millionaire Peter Montagu Meyer, girlfriend of Lucan.

DOMINIC ELWES. Painter. He had known Lucan for ten years and saw a lot of him at the Clermont.

JAMES FOX. Old-Etonian. Journalist and long-time friend of Lucan.

JAMES GOLDSMITH. Old Etonian. Businessman, descended from the Goldschmidt family of Frankfurt Jews. Friend and confidant of Lucan.

CAROLINE HILL. Secretary. Had known Lucan since 1956 and was giving him weekly piano lessons.

GREVILLE HOWARD. Banker. Clermont regular, a friend of Lucan and living in his mews house at 5 Eaton Row. Worked for Goldsmith.

CHRISTINA SHAND KYDD. Younger sister of Veronica.

WILLIAM SHAND KYDD. Brother-in-law of Veronica.

DANIEL MEINERTZHAGEN. Old Etonian. Company director, son of the chairman of Lazards bank. Like Lucan, a house gambler at the Clermont.

STEPHEN RAPHAEL. Stockbroker. Managed Lucan's investments. Experienced bridge and poker player, a father figure to Lucan.

IAN MAXWELL-SCOTT. Member of one of the country's oldest Catholic families, related to the Duke of Norfolk. Gambler, helped Aspinall establish the Clermont.

SUSAN MAXWELL-SCOTT. Qualified barrister. Daughter of Sir Andrew Clark, QC. Mother of six children.

MICHAEL STOOP. Top backgammon player, friend of Lucan for nearly twenty years.

SELIM ZILKHA. Chairman of Mothercare children's clothes chain. Member of the St James Club, knew Lucan socially.

Under the banking laws it wasn't enough to simply ask them to open up Lucan's accounts for inspection. It was necessary to get permission from magistrates to probe into his financial affairs. The first time an application was made to Bow Street court it was refused and valuable time was lost. A second application had to be made under the Bankers' Books Evidence Act. This time Roy Ranson was successful in convincing magistrate Mr Evelyn Russell that the only intention was to help in the search for Lucan by seeing if there had been any withdrawals from his accounts. Roy Ranson said afterwards: 'We are not interested in his financial affairs. We just hope that they may help us to trace his movements. If an entry shows that cash was withdrawn from a certain branch after the murder then we have somewhere to start looking.'

When Lucan's finances were finally sorted out it was estimated he had total debts of £74,000, a tidy sum when his income from a trust fund was only about £7,000 a year gross, reduced to £5,500 after tax, while his outgoings were some £12,000 net. He had overdrafts with four banks, £2,841 with Coutts, £4,379 with Lloyds, £5,667 with the Midland and £1,290 with the National Westminster. Among his big debts was £10,000 owing to the Clermont, his second home for so many years. Lucan had been borrowing heavily from other sources, too: £3,000 from the Edgware Trust; £3,000 from Selim Zilkha; £4,000 from his mother, the Dowager Countess; and other sums from tolerant friends. Apart from his debts he was giving his wife £40 a week and paying £25 to Sandra Rivett. He was in a financial mess.

Dr Margaret Pereira, senior scientific officer in the biology division of Scotland Yard's forensic science laboratory, was known to us simply as 'Miss Murder'. She was an acknowledged international expert in the field, having helped pioneer a method of analysing even the tiniest spots of dried blood. At No. 46 this particular skill wasn't called upon as there was a profusion of blood samples to work on, too much if anything. There were heavy blood stains on the floor. It was on the ground floor walls and ceiling and those in the basement, some of it containing hair. Spots of blood had been thrown off the lead pipe to cause a radiating directional pattern of stains as it was repeatedly raised and brought down with sickening ferocity. As it was used to attack both women, there was a third AB blood group, apparently made up of a mixture of the blood of both of them and also found on the floor of the abandoned car.

What was needed was to separate the blood of Sandra Rivett from that of Veronica in order to determine where their respective attacks took place, bearing in mind Lucan would say he saw through the window the fight going on in the basement. From the trajectory of the splashes on the walls she was able to define the exact point where Sandra was attacked in the basement. The majority of the blood in the basement was that of Sandra and that in the hallway above that of Veronica, but some of it had been carried about between the two areas, either by blood-spattered Lucan or on the shoes of the posse of police officers who had first invaded the scene. The findings of Dr Pereira were enough to persuade me they fitted into the pattern as we understood the attacks to have been carried out, but they were open to a different interpretation by a wily defence counsel. I could envisage Dr Pereira being closely questioned by Lucan's doubtless top and expensive QC on how Sandra's blood was found to be smeared on Veronica's dress and how Veronica's shoes had Sandra's blood on them? It would muddy the water, sow seeds of doubt in the minds of the jury and perhaps convince them Lucan's defence was the truth and there was an unknown third party involved.

On the day before the murder, Wednesday, 6 November, Lucan did nothing to arouse suspicions that he was planning to embark on a momentous course of action that was to dramatically change his life and that of a number of other people in a few seconds of frenzied violence.

In the morning he visited a friend, Caroline Hill, at her Kensington home in Old Church Street, for a weekly piano lesson. He had known her since 1956 and she had taught the Lucan children to play the piano. Caroline told us that Lucan had many times told her about his wife's odd behaviour and had sought her advice on living with a mentally disturbed person.

The afternoon found Lucan picking up some laundry and a suit from a cleaning firm in Lansdown Road before he turned up again at the Haywood-Hill bookshop in Curzon Street at 4.45 p.m. and bought the book about Greek shipping millionaires we found in his flat.

Lucan rounded off what appeared to be a perfectly ordinary day at a dinner party given by Selim Zilkha at his flat in Portland Place. He arrived at about 7.15 p.m. and stayed late, spending the evening playing backgammon and bridge with other male guests.

If Lucan had evil on his mind he hid it well. Nobody said he was other than his normal self. At Zilkha's party he had even offered to deliver a parcel on Friday or Saturday, which would have been after the murder. Either he made the offer as part of the pattern of establishing an alibi or the decision to kill Veronica was taken on the morning of the day itself when he felt everything was exactly right.

On Wednesday, 13 November, just six days after she was savagely assaulted, doctors gave Veronica permission to leave St George's Hospital to make what the press described as a 'dramatic court dash'. Although she wasn't fully recovered she insisted on going to the High Court for a hearing over the future of her three children. Veronica travelled to the Law Courts in the Strand in a Rover police car, sitting in the back flanked by Sgt Forsyth and another detective, her taut face and haunted expression clearly showing the strain of her ordeal. In hospital she had been visisted by her sister Christina and Lucan's brother, Hugh Bingham. Sgt Forsyth had told me what happened had been most strange. When Christina had entered the room they had not clasped one another as might be expected of blood sisters in the circumstances. Nor had there been any warmth between the two. The meeting was cold. Veronica left hospital to face the world and a battery of photographers wearing dark glasses, a turban hat concealing the scars on her head.

The hearing was arranged for 9.45 a.m. in the Family Division before Mr Justice Rees, the same judge who had previously granted her custody. It was quickly opened and adjourned before Veronica arrived. She was driven to Gerald Road for further questioning before going back to brave the nightmare of walking once again through the door of 46 Lower Belgrave Street. While she waited at home without her children, Veronica was comforted by a woman who had befriended her, Mary-Geraldine O'Donnell, known as Mary-O. She was also visited by Father Desmond Tillyer, the priest from her church, St Peter's, in Eaton Square.

When the hearing was resumed two days later on Friday, Veronica had to plead once again through her legal representative to retain custody of the children against opposition from the Lucan family. The hearing *in camera* lasted for half-an-hour before lawyers for the two sides adjourned to thrash out a solution in the judge's private rooms. The custody battle took place in strict secrecy and Veronica was smuggled out a private door afterwards. With the custody ordeal over Veronica looked happier and was much photographed in a mini wool coat and matching dress, this time not wearing sunglasses, the stitches from the wound on her forehead clearly visible beneath her hat.

Mr Justice Rees took the rare step of approving a statement for the Official Receiver, Mr Norman Turner, to read out to reporters called into the courtroom. It said: 'The judge has authorized the following statement concerning the children of Lord and Lady Lucan. They are wards of court. There has been a hearing in chambers, as a result of which an order has been made approving arrangements for them. The children will be living with their mother. It has been ordered that, except for the contents of this statement, the arrangements and the order shall not be published. The parties are united in the hope that the children will now be allowed to resume their lives undisturbed and they will now be spared any further publicity.'

The children had been taken on the day after the drama first began to the home of Lucan's younger sister, Lady Sarah 'Sally' Gibbs, wife of the Reverend William Gibbs, in the Northamptonshire village of Guilsborough. The children were staying with their cousins at the vicarage of St Ethelred's Church where William was the vicar. Sally and Willian were doing their best to keep the children from seeing newspapers and the television news, but it was difficult to ignore the reporters and photographers laying siege to the old house. Sally had faced the difficult task of telling the children as much as it was felt necessary for them to know about the events that had taken place. William told the press he would wait for confirmation from the Official Solicitor about the result of the court case and he did not know when the children would be handed over to Veronica.

9   The Perfect Murder

In January 1973 Lucan finally split up from Veronica after a long period of bickering and he moved for a time into the nearby mews cottage in Eaton Row. If he was upset at the separation and his return to life as a bachelor he was determined not to show it. The following month he flew to Mexico to join friends celebrating the 40th birthday of international wheeler-dealer Jimmy Goldsmith at the time he was wisely dumping stock and going liquid in advance of the impending crash. Among those invited to the extended house party in Acapulco was their mutual friend Dominic Elwes, court jester of the Clermont habitués. Lucan and Elwes were pictured together sunbathing and sharing a joke. They were good fun together, actress Joanna Lumley recalling in her book *Stare Back and Smile* how she spent an enjoyable supper with the pair when they were in high spirits.

Unfortunately as it was to turn out, Lucan was also snapped on camera in Acapulco drinking at a table with a group of friends. Lucan was sitting alongside Lady Annabel Birley, the youngest daughter of the Marquess of Londonderry, who had married Mark Birley when she was nineteen but had become the long-time mistress of Jimmy Goldsmith. One of the coloured photographs showed willowy brunette Annabel with her arm resting on Lucan's shoulder as she looked into his sunburned face. It was a harmless enough snapshot, but one that was to lead ultimately to the death of Dominic Elwes in the tragic wake of the Lucan saga.

By the time I first entered the hallowed portals of the Clermont Club its glory days as a bastion of snobbery with John Aspinall were over. He was a remarkable man, one of life's non-conformists who enjoyed bending rules and was largely responsible for bringing about the change in the gambling laws with his floating chemmy games. He was also a natural publicity-gatherer, first getting his name into the newspapers following a brawl at a celebrity film premiere party at Les Ambassadeurs nightclub in which Robert Mitchum had got involved as a bystander. The fight was over a bouncing cheque Aspinall had been given at one of his early gambling parties when he had little money and it caused him problems paying out the winners.

Aspinall had discovered under the terms of the 1854 Gaming Act private gambling was permissible provided it did not occur more than twice at the same venue. The answer was simple: don't hold games twice at the same address. He took advantage of this simple loophole in the mid-1950s by arranging games at different addresses around Mayfair. They became popular with titled landowners who formed the country's biggest gamblers and he would make his profit by taking a percentage of the money bet. Whoever won and lost Aspinall would emerge a winner, the indolent rich apparently prepared to be relieved of their money provided it was done with panache.

Apart from the chemin-de-fer itself the games attracted a discerning circle like the Earl of Derby and the Duke of Devonshire because of the food provided by Aspinall's mother, who had become Lady Osborne after her second marriage and was known as Lady O. When she took the tenancy of a Hyde Park flat for regular sessions it was raided and a score of people from illustrious families suffered the ignominy of being carted off to the police station. Aspers was charged with keeping a common gaming-house and Lady O with permitting her premises to be used for the purpose of unlawful gaming. The subsequent trial at the London Sessions in 1958 collapsed with the old gaming law made to look ridiculous and the judge ordered the jury to return 'not guilty' verdicts. Within three years what was called 'Aspinall's Law' resulted in the new legislation and a shower of casinos, not at all what the government had intended.

When Aspinall opened the Clermont he created Europe's most sophisticated club by lovingly restoring a gem of a property built by William Kent in the 1740s, his only surviving town house in London. He named it after Lord Clermont, an eighteenth century gambler known as the 'Father of the Turf' and friend of the Prince of Wales. No expense was spared on the restoration of the house and the result was magnificent, its marble staircase rising through four floors and the splendid Grand Saloon on the first floor looking as if it was designed to house gaming tables. Disaster almost struck as the club was about to open when Aspinall lost all his money with the Wall Street crash of May 1962, but he recovered from the setback in typical fashion by raising the funding through friends prepared to back the venture.

After a decade Aspinall became disenchanted with gambling for a while and sold the club to concentrate on animal conservation. At Howletts, his zoo near Canterbury in Kent, he was involved in breeding gorillas and he also bought and restored Port Lympne near Ashford as a zoo, buying in his inimitable cavalier style at a time his finances had taken a hammering in the 1973–4 slump. His departure from the Clermont was greatly mourned by close friends who had benefited from his loyalty and patronage, in particular Lucan. It was at the Clermont where Lucan spent much of his time, so it was among his friends at the club where we expected to find the clues to his outlandish plot to kill Veronica. There was a helpful sign pinned up which read: '*If Lord Lucan comes in will he please ring 999 as someone wants to interview him.*'

With the custody conflict settled it was decided Veronica and the children would be better off out of London. There was no sign of a waning interest by the voracious media, and it was obvious every time the family stepped outside the door they would be snapped by the waiting paparazzi. The decision was taken they should go to the farmhouse of a friend of Veronica's near Torbay in Devon. Two of the children, Frances and George, were taken in a car by DC Sally Bower, Camilla staying behind because she had a cold. Veronica travelled with Sgt Forsyth on the train from Paddington in their own compartment. They were already at the house with a senior uniformed officer from the Devon and Cornwall Constabulary when the car with the children drove up and they stepped out. Sgt Forsyth introduced them to the senior officer. 'How do you do, Lord George,' he said. 'Don't call me Lord, call me George,' said the seven-year-old boy with the sort of confidence that comes from generations of aristocratic breeding.

On their return a new nanny, Christabel Martin, moved in to look after the children. She had looked after them previously as a stand-in for Sandra Rivett and said she was a friend of Veronica's. Like Sandra, Christabel was twenty-nine. She stayed only three weeks before adding her name to the long list of ex-nannies. Ten years later Christabel was to meet a violent end herself, strangled by her husband, her body cut up and the pieces dumped around London in plastic bags. Her husband, Nicholas Boyce, was sentenced at the Old Bailey in October, 1985, to six years for manslaughter.

Lucan's girlfriend, 22-year-old Chelsea ex-deb Andrina 'Andy' Colquhoun, denied to the press she was his lover, saying she liked him but regarded him just as a great friend. They had first met six months earlier at a lunch party at the Clermont and he was interested in her expertise as a photographer. While he had been separated from his wife for nearly two years he was still a married man with three children and she had not wanted to get involved with him in that situation. She told us Lucan had a preoccupation and love for his children. On 7 November Andrina rang Lucan at his flat and he was vague about his plans for that evening, suggesting dinner but asking her to confirm it on the telephone in the afternoon. When she phoned in the afternoon there was no answer. She had looked for him at the Clermont and at his flat but there was no trace of either Lucan or his Mercedes so she drove down to Kent for a green-wellie weekend shooting party.

Andrina said in an interview reported in the *Daily Mail*: 'When we went out, perhaps once or twice a week, we would invariably have dinner at the Clermont and then go downstairs to Annabel's nightclub for a drink and a dance. We talked about lots of things, mainly current events, what people we knew were doing, but we never discussed his wife – or gambling. When I went out with him he never left me sitting around to go off gambling. I have been out with other people in the last few months as well. I liked Lord Lucan a lot. As far as I know he did not take out any other girls. Things might have been different if he was not a married man.'

We were naturally interested in tracking down witnesses who could tell us what Lucan had been doing earlier on the day of the murder. By tracing his movements and demeanour we hoped to be in a position to tell if Lucan was a man who planned a premeditated murder or had acted impulsively. Nor could we rule out his own version of events that he was entirely innocent, butting in to rescue Veronica as she was being attacked and fleeing only because he knew nobody would believe his story of a 'traumatic night of unbelievable coincidences'. It seemed unlikely, but after many years as a detective I knew anything was possible and it would be dangerous not to keep an open mind.

At 4 p.m. we were able to place Lucan at the John Harley chemist shop in Lower Belgrave Street. Pharmacist Alfred Simons said Lucan asked him to identify a capsule and he told him it was Limbutral, a drug used for treating nervous complaints. Several times over the previous two or three years Lucan had been into the shop and enquired about anti-depressant and tranquillizing drugs. He thought they were drugs which had been prescribed for Lucan's wife.

Michael Hicks Beach, an Old-Etonian literary agent and gambling friend of Lucan, revealed to our investigators that Lucan called him on the telephone at about 4.45 p.m. and asked if he would edit an article he had been asked to write for an Oxford magazine. He said he would and arrived at Lucan's Elizabeth Street flat between 6.30 and 7 p.m. Lucan apologized for asking him over at such short notice but explained he wanted his help with the piece he had written on gambling. While they were working on the article Lucan had telephoned the Clermont and booked a table for dinner that evening. When they had finished Lucan drove him back to his home at Oakley Gardens in a car that wasn't his Mercedes and matched the description of the borrowed Ford Corsair. Lucan had dropped him off outside his house just before 8 p.m., suggesting they might have lunch or dinner together over the weekend. He said Lucan had been wearing a pullover over a polo-necked shirt and an old pair of flannels and had been in a relaxed mood.

Two people we turned up at the Clermont had information of particular interest. One was the assistant restaurant manager Andrew Demetriou, the other the 'linkman' who parked the cars, William 'Billy' Edgson.

Andrew Demetriou told us on the night of 7 November he went on duty at 7.30 p.m. and about 8 p.m. he received a telephone call from Lucan. He had asked to speak to the restaurant manager and, when he was told he was not available, he booked a table for four at 11 p.m., mentioning it was to follow a theatre visit. Greville Howard and the theatre party arrived between 10.45 and 11 p.m. after seeing *Cole* at the Mermaid Theatre and asked for a fifth chair to be put at the table for Lucan, but he failed to show up. What Andrew Demetriou said tied in nicely with what Michael Hicks Beach recalled about Lucan making the call to book the table while he was at his flat.

Billy Edgson said Lucan turned up outside the Clermont at about 8.45 p.m., winding down the window of his car and asking: 'Anybody in the club?' When he was told 'None of the usual crowd, Sir,' he commented 'Thank you very much' and drove off, saying he would be back. What was intriguing was that Edgson believed Lucan had been driving his Mercedes. The Clermont was only about a mile away from Lower Belgrave Street and at that time of night it would take under ten minutes to drive, not a lot more even if he went to Elizabeth Street to switch cars. I was sceptical about the varying times given, knowing the notorious inability of witnesses to be exact. An error of a few minutes could make all the difference to Lucan being able to have plenty of time to let himself into No. 46 with his latchkey and secrete himself in the basement. Unfortunately time discrepancies would open the door for a defence lawyer at Lucan's trial to seek to discredit the prosecution case. All that would be in the future. First we had to catch the slippery Lucan who, up until the Criminal Justice Act of 1948, would have been able to claim the right to be tried in the House of Lords by his fellow peers and, if found guilty, to be hung at the end of a silken rope. That would have been something to see, but it hadn't happened for more than 200 years.

What the evidence of the witnesses clearly suggested was Lucan had been at great pains to concoct a cast-iron alibi for the evening of 7 November. He asked Michael Hicks Beach to his flat at short notice and, while he was there, telephoned the Clermont to book a table. With a meticulous eye to detail he obviously hadn't thought it enough to rely on the memory of a busy restaurant manager to establish the time of the booking. Then he drove to the Clermont in his Mercedes shortly before the murder and deliberately spoke to Billy Edgson, the linkman who parked and collected cars. He had known Billy for a number of years and he would surely remember their short conversation about who was in the club. It was not necessary to establish a precise alibi for every minute of the evening. The beauty of the plan was that Veronica would supposedly

The Perfect Murder

disappear from her home unseen and nobody would know exactly at what time she left. If the nanny returned home late and went straight to bed it could be the following morning before she was missed.

It may even have been Lucan's intention to drive by the house after leaving the Clermont with his friends, calling in on some invented pretext or other because he might have been worried about the children being on their own. He would feign surprise at Veronica not being there and look after the children until Sandra Rivett returned home. Either way, many people disappeared in London all the time, and with Veronica's history of psychiatric treatment her sudden and unexplained absence would not arouse suspicions of foul play. There would not be more than a cursory investigation – she would be circulated as a missing person and added to the lengthy files. Friends would express their deepest sympathy to Lucan, saying it confirmed what he had been saying all along, that Veronica was mentally unstable. She could have gone anywhere, might even have wandered off and thrown herself into the dark waters of the River Thames.

At all times as he went calmly about establishing his alibi Lucan had been careful to be his normal self, not giving anyone any outward sign of agitation or excitement. Behind his poker-faced façade his adrenalin must have been flowing as he embarked on the greatest gamble of his life. He staked everything on his carefully devised plan, unaware the cards were already stacked against him. Before the midnight hour he would have blood on his hands, a fugitive on the run from the law.

It was Greville Howard who gave us a vital piece of evidence to show the murder was premeditated and that Lucan had drawn up a blueprint to kill Veronica with the detailed attention of a military operation. I regarded Howard, a cousin of the Earl of Suffolk, as an extreme right-winger. He was private secretary to Enoch Powell for four years after he made his controversial 'rivers of blood' speech on immigration at Birmingham in 1968. In his statement he divulged a conversation he had with Lucan some three months earlier in the year when they were drinking together at the Elizabeth Street flat. Lucan spoke about his financial affairs, saying he could see no way out of his problems. What was worrying him was the fact his children might see him end up in court as a bankrupt. 'It would be much easier,' Lucan said in his cups, 'to get rid of Veronica and dump her body in the Solent.' When Greville Howard rebuked him, saying it would be far worse if the children saw him in court accused of murder rather than as a bankrupt, Lucan stated ominously: 'I wouldn't get caught.' At the time Greville Howard dismissed the remarks as drunken ramblings and took little notice. But Lucan was either gifted with supernatural powers of foresight or he wasn't speaking in jest. The idea of solving his worsening financial plight by slaying Veronica was already taking shape.

On the face of it, Lucan planned what looked in his eyes to be the perfect murder. He spent some time adding to the already established groundwork that Veronica's mental state was deteriorating. Next he borrowed an old car, nondescript and less conspicuous than his own Mercedes, to remove Veronica's body for disposal. He either picked up two pieces of lead piping or cut a longer piece nearly in the middle to give differing lengths. Both he wrapped in adhesive tape, like a golfer selecting a club, testing which one felt the most balanced and comfortable in his gloved hand.

Having ascertained from Frances that Thursday was nanny Sandra Rivett's day off, he ostentatiously arranged an alibi for the night. Before setting out he removed everything from his pockets, not wanting to be encumbered or to inadvertently drop anything at the scene that might identify him. He left all the items on the bed alongside the clothes he had laid out ready for a quick change when the deed was completed.

After showing his face to Billy Edgson at the Clermont he returned and swapped his Mercedes for the Ford Corsair, leaving it as close as possible to the basement steps at No. 46. He may even have parked the Ford there earlier to ensure he had a parking space near the steps, not wanting to carry the body too far along the street. He then let himself quietly into the house with his own key, carrying the mail-bag we believed he purloined from the Clermont and wearing the old brown overcoat over his sweater.

Making his way to the basement he took out the light bulb and waited in the dark for Veronica to descend the stairs to her doom, exhilarated like all gamblers by danger, a fear of discovery. When he had killed his wife with blows to the head like a hammer on an anvil he would place her in the mail-bag and drag it up the basement steps to the waiting car. The main element of risk would come as he bundled the mail-bag into the boot of the car, but it was a chance he would have to take. Unfortunately, there was no rear entrance to the house. As it was a wet night it was unlikely many people would be abroad in Lower Belgrave Street and the odds were against anyone looking out of a window. If he peered out through the basement railings, he could make sure there was nobody about or any cars passing before he crossed the pavement and tipped the bag into the boot. It wouldn't be easy, but Veronica was small and thin, weighing little more than a child, so he would manage it.

He would then go back into the house through the basement, locking the kitchen door behind him, and let himself out the front door, again checking to see the coast was clear. Once he had driven away he would park the Ford Corsair near his flat, quickly change his clothes and drive to the Clermont in his Mercedes to meet his friends for dinner. He would have all weekend to dispose of Veronica's body at his convenience, possibly by taking it to the South Coast and dropping it weighted down into the Solent as suggested to Greville Howard. Veronica would have vanished and his problems would be over once and for all, or at least until his passion for gambling again brought him to the point of ruination.

Unfortunately, as with the best laid plans of mice and men, it was to go catastrophically wrong. Because she had changed her day off, it was Sandra Rivett and not Veronica who walked down as Lucan waited sweating in his overcoat in the basement, skulking in the deep shadow at the side of the stairs. And he wasn't to know the powerful blows he brought crashing down on his victim's skull would result in a cascade of blood as her scalp burst open. From that moment, even before Veronica arrived calling 'Sandra, Sandra' and he realized in mind-numbing terror he had dispatched the wrong woman, his carefully devised plan was already hopelessly in tatters. If Veronica had been killed as intended the bloodbath in the kitchen would have screamed out that she had met a terrible fate and hadn't just walked out of the house on her own in a demented state. Even if Lucan had spent all night cleaning up the mess, abandoning the part of his alibi that required him eating supper at the Clermont, he would have faced an impossible task. The cloying, sickly-smelling blood was everywhere.

10 Man on the Run

The reel-to-reel tapes taken from Lucan's flat were not what I was expecting at all. Unlike the cassettes they were not recordings of garbled conversations he had taped with his wife. They were recordings of Adolf Hitler's pre-World War Two rabble-rousing speeches to his Nazi supporters at mass rallies, like the famous one at Nuremberg I had seen on old newsreels. Just why Lucan wanted to listen to the German führer's rantings wasn't clear, but if they told us nothing else the tapes confirmed his politics were to the far right. His undisguised opinions were deeply entrenched in the hang 'em and flog 'em school. This was something that was already becoming apparent from the interviews we were having with his pals at the Clermont and Portland Club who shared his concern about the worsening state of the nation. There were fears the pillars of society were crumbling in the face of the Communist threat and the very fabric of British society was in grave danger of being swept away in a tide of worker revolution.

The year began with industrial unrest and a three-day working week caused by a miners' strike that finally forced Prime Minister Ted Heath to hold a 'Who Rules Britain?' general election in February. There was no clear majority for any party and it was Harold Wilson who was able to cobble together a minority Labour government. Viewed from the closeted comfort of London's clubland the reds were out from under the beds and the wave of strikes throughout 1974 was seen as a sign of national disintegration. Harold Wilson struggled through to October when he called another election with a promise of arbitration and conciliation services to settle disputes, securing only a tiny majority because of internal squabbling over Europe. In his manifesto, Tory Leader Ted Heath warned economic and political dangers facing Britain were the worst since the war, a fear echoed over dinner tables in the clubs Lucan frequented. Apart from losing three out of four elections Ted Heath suffered another setback. In September his beloved racing yacht *Morning Cloud* sank off the South Coast in a force 9 gale with the loss of two crewmen while he was in America. The yacht was found eight days later and taken into Shoreham, a total wreck. Would a similar wrecked boat be found in the channel with the body of Lucan inside?

It wasn't only in Britain that there was turmoil in 1974. In Spain Prime Minister Admiral Luis Carero Blanco was assassinated when his car was blown up. Archbishop Makarios fled to Britain from Cyprus when Greek officers of the National Guard staged a coup, returning to a divided island following a Turkish invasion. Argentina's President Juan Peron died only a year after returning from an 18-year exile, handing over power to his one-time cabaret dancer wife Isabel. In Spain General Spinola resigned under pressure from radical leaders of the Armed Force Movement after a five-month spell as president, replaced by General Francisco da Costa Gomez. Valery Giscard d'Estaing became president of France after the death of Georges Pompidou from a mystery illness. Willy Brandt resigned as West German Chancellor following a spy scandal and Helmut Schmidt took over. In Ethiopia, Haile Selassie, King of Kings, the 'Lion of Judah', was deposed in a military coup after ruling since 1930.

With talk of a national strike looming in Britain there was a suggestion from Colonel David Stirling, a man known to Lucan who had been involved in the civil war in the Yemen in the mid-1960s, for the formation of a private army to take over to restore law and order. It was a concept Lucan supported, fitting in well with his notion of a wage-slave proletariat kept firmly in its place by a superior but benevolent ruling class. Lucan made no secret of his right-wing attitudes, sounding off in front of strangers about everything from worthless foreigners to repatriating immigrants. Skinheads weren't exactly Lucan's social cup of tea, but no doubt he supported their aim when they demonstrated that summer in Red Lion Square against an amnesty being granted to illegal immigrants. The National Front demo in Holborn resulted in a violent battle with left wingers which mounted police had to sort out. One student died in hospital from his injuries. To me the mental image of Lucan sitting alone in his flat listening to the fascist ravings of Hitler was both bizarre and sad.

Right from the start there were wild rumours circulating about the mental state of Veronica and how her weird behaviour had driven her long-suffering husband to take drastic action. It was difficult to tell if the stories were just harmless dinner table gossip or if they were part of a deliberate whispering campaign by Lucan's supporters to protect him and lay the foundation for his defence should he be caught. It may even have been a direct result of Lucan spreading stories himself at the time he was trying to convince one and all Veronica was going round the twist.

Whatever the reason, the stories circulated widely, becoming more outrageous as they were embellished in the telling. What they all seemed to have in common was that Lucan was the innocent party and Veronica was a neurotic nutter. They may have been intentionally put about to blacken her name. As far as I know not one of the rumours was true but I heard them repeated many times, told with conviction, the details varying as they were passed from mouth to mouth. However obscene, people seemed prepared to believe even the most preposterous lies being spread about Veronica. It was hardly surprising she was awarded the tag of the most disliked woman in London, even by people who had never set eyes on her.

I was particularly amused by the monstrous yarns about the terrible fate of a black kitten which devoted father Lucan supposedly bought and gave to his children as a loving present. Wicked Veronica had reportedly sliced the head off the luckless pussycat and impaled it on the railings outside her house. Or, in other versions, she chopped it up or tore it apart with her bare hands, returning it to dismayed Lucan by stuffing the dismembered furry bits through the letter box of his flat. Before performing this cruel act, crazed Veronica had seemingly been fond of serving up the cat's excreta to her children on dinner plates.

It was certainly true Veronica had a black cat called *Sooty*, but it was still alive and kicking after the murder and much fussed over. Sandra Rivett had introduced her cat *Tara* to the house as well. What was true was that the cats had made a mess on the ground floor of the house, presumably because they had been unable to get out to do their business in the back garden. There was one gruesome story about the cats that *was* true. One of them was found by officers first on the scene of the murder. It was lapping blood from the pool on the basement floor and had to be shooed away. When Veronica went off to stay in Torbay, I arranged for the two cats to be placed in a cattery at Hampstead and we were presented with a bill for £40. There wasn't a dog to be looked after. According to the rumour mongers this much-loved pet of the children had also been dispatched by Veronica along with the cat.

One of the more malicious rumours in circulation as the vicious campaign against Veronica gathered momentum was that she and Sandra Rivett were engaged in a passionate lesbian love affair. We looked into this closely, believing an attempt would be made at any subsequent trial to attack Sandra's character by suggesting she was actually the intended victim of an unknown murderer. While Sandra was a lively girl and had been involved in many affairs over the years, there was not the slightest hint that any of them were other than heterosexual. Sandra had only been working at the Lucan household for a few weeks and we were convinced there was nothing more than a normal friendly relationship between two women who shared a common bond in that they were both separated from their husbands.

As the rumour machine went into top gear, Veronica was supposed to have forced her young children to shape men's penises out of Plasticine. She was said to have thrown a glass of wine over a woman in one of many embarrassing drunken rages at the Clermont, though I asked extensively at the club and was never able to identify the recipient of her violent anger. Lucan himself, meanwhile, had apparently taken himself straight off to Howletts after leaving Susan Maxwell-Scott's and persuaded his good friend John Aspinall to feed his mortal remains to his tigers after he had done the decent thing and killed himself. The delighted tigers had chomped him up, bones and all, so not one scrap of the honourable 7th Earl of Lucan remained to further besmirch the family history. It was a colourful tale, spoiled only by the fact that Aspinall pointed out his tigers were fed once a week and would only have eaten human flesh if they were starving.

* * *

There is, unfortunately, always competition between police forces, an argument some would say in favour of a national body. It is inevitable the local lads are going to resent outsiders invading their patch, especially when heavies from the Old Bill turn up to investigate crimes. Prior to the Magistrates' Courts Act of 1952, it was necessary to be sworn in as a constable in an area outside your own where you wanted to operate. It was a tiresome business that was particularly irksome for Flying Squad officers on the track of pickpockets at racecourses dotted around the country. Fortunately the practice had ended by the time I headed off for Newhaven, but a parochial attitude still existed among older officers in those forces which bordered the Metropolitan Police area. In Sussex the relationship with the local officers, including the CID at Newhaven and Seaford, was excellent, but the Chief Constable wasn't too pleased. He didn't complain formally, but it was clear he wasn't a happy man. He felt any requests for information about police activity taking place in his backyard should be directed solely through his press relations office. That was all very well, but Fleet Street didn't operate through artificial administrative boundaries. Reporters had virtually total freedom to go where they liked and speak to whoever they wanted. Ever anxious to keep the Lucan saga on the boil they turned up in force and fresh headlines shrieked DIVERS HUNT FOR LUCAN in the *Evening Standard* and DIVERS SEARCH FOR LUCAN in the *Evening News*.

It was obvious the area around Newhaven was not going to be easy to search. I knew the town well, having lived for a short while at Seaford when I left school, and I joined the Royal Naval Volunteer Reserve at Newhaven until I was conscripted for National Service into the Royal Navy. Apart from the port and the marina with hundreds of boats berthed for the winter, there was a long stretch of coastline with isolated coves and the river to be scoured for a body. Ashore it was just as bad, with the windswept downland hills above the port covered in impenetrable gorse.

We were particularly interested in an old Napoleonic fort to the west of the harbour, an area honeycombed with passages and flooded chambers less than a mile from where the Ford Corsair was discovered at Norman Road. To effectively comb the whole area required a massive operation which would stretch our resources, so Roy Ranson and I decided it would be a good idea to call on the Army for help. It was a proposal which didn't go down well with the Chief Constable when he heard about it, but I went to the Army barracks at Aldershot to discuss it with senior military officers. It was agreed the exercise would provide worthwhile training for the troops, but in the end the plan fell through. We didn't have the necessary logistical resources to transport and feed a large number of men.

What we decided to do was use all the available manpower we could drum up from the Sussex and Met forces, which gave us a total of fourteen tracker dogs. Two German shepherds from Scotland Yard were specially trained to find buried bodies and had been used in the Sinai desert to find bodies in the sand after the Arab-Israeli war. We had a similar number of divers, nine from the Sussex Task Force and five from Scotland Yard who arrived in their own truck and were booked into the Eversley Hotel in Seaford. Even the two police horses from Brighton, Justin and Roland, were roped in to assist in the search. I travelled down on Sunday, 24 November, and worked out a plan with the local man, Detective Inspector Cyril Price, on how and where the divers and dog teams could best be used. Inspector Price was interviewed on television soon after the car was found and said Lucan could be anywhere. 'I cannot understand why this car should be found down here,' he said.

The frogmen had both a difficult and dangerous task, risking being sucked into a whirlpool known as 'The Hole' at the mouth of the River Ouse where bodies had previously been found. They rummaged about in the freezing harbour with its strong currents and underwater obstructions, jagged metal pylons sticking up from the seabed threatening to tear their flesh. The divers had to work largely by feel because there was zero visibility in the muddy water, but their efforts were unrewarded. There were no bloated bodies to be found floating in the river or caught up on the piles, either in the harbour or the Cresta Marina.

On dry land the dog handlers, working under Sgt John Bostock from the Met and Sgt Ron Withers from Brighton, weren't having an easy time either among blackthorn bushes and spiky gorse. It was head-high in places and scratched hands and faces. The dogs didn't like the painful thorns that stuck into them as they nosed into the thick, sodden bushes and had to be carefully pulled out when the mud was washed from their fur afterwards. The teams searched the cliffs between deserted caravans at holiday parks, picnic sites and beauty spots. A big area had to be covered, as far as Peacehaven in the west and stretching out in the east to the high Beachy Head cliffs notorious for suicide jumpers. One body was discovered hanging from a tree, but it was clearly not Lucan, and human bones found later near the River Ouse were identified as those of a judge who had gone missing nearly ten years earlier.

The macabre finds enabled their respective files to be closed, but there was no sign Lucan had camped out in a derelict building or had ended his life among the brambles on the windswept cliffs. Given the size of the job we could have used hundreds of soldiers to explore every location within a five-mile radius of Newhaven. I got an impression of the scale of the task when I was taken on board the Sussex police launch *MV Norfolk* for a trip along the coast from Chichester. There was miles of coastline with thousands of boats, an impossible mission for one launch to effectively police. Any one of the boats or the buildings along the headland might be concealing Lucan or his dead body.

With the resources at our disposal we managed to cover the obvious sites and I was reasonably satisfied Lucan was not there to be found unless he had crawled into the middle of a thicket or gone to earth in a hole in the ground. If he had deliberately hidden away in an animal burrow and killed himself, it could be a long time before his body was found. I thought it was a remote prospect Lucan would have headed for the gale-lashed hills as it was well before dawn and pitch dark when the car was parked. Besides, I wasn't happy with the idea that he would travel all the way to the Sussex coast or even out in the English Channel to do away with himself. If he was intent on self-destruction after the blood-chilling events in the basement of 46 Lower Belgrave Street I reasoned it would have happened sooner rather than later. I felt the further he got away from the scene of the crime, the less likely it was he would commit suicide.

While the search was going on I spent the week investigating the other possibility, that Lucan had been to Newhaven and had escaped to France, either on the ferry or in one of the small boats on the river or tied up in Cresta Marina. I spoke to the people who were responsible for the marina and officials at the yacht club. The records of the watch tower whose staff monitored boats arriving and leaving the port were examined, as was the Sealink car manifest. I spoke to officers of British Transport Police as the ferries that crossed the Channel to france were British Rail ships, and to Special Branch officers who were on permanent duty at the port. Everywhere I went I drew a total blank. Newhaven was a small town centred on the port and virtually lifeless and deserted in November. Anyone staying in bed-and-breakfast accommodation or even having a drink in a pub would have been remembered. If the urbane Lucan had stayed there, or even walked about, he would have needed to be the Invisible Man not to be noticed by somebody.

What I did find interesting at Newhaven was the site where Lucan's car was found in Norman Road. Anyone arriving along the road from Lewes would have come to a cross-roads on the outskirts of the town. If they were just looking for the nearest sidestreet to abandon the car, they would drive on a short distance and come straight to Norman Road. If, on the other hand, they were intending to make for the port or the marina they would drive a lot nearer to avoid being seen walking some distance along the road. It struck me the Ford Corsair had been left at the first available spot and whoever placed it there immediately drove off in an accompanying vehicle. It could have been Lucan who drove the blood-stained car. It would have made sense as his fingerprints were already on it. They weren't to know that the rear view mirror of a car, where people take a firm hold with their thumb to adjust it, was probably the only place where a decent print could be lifted. Just as easily it could have been somebody else wearing gloves.

Given the time lapse after Susan Maxwell-Scott said Lucan left her house to when the car was first spotted at Norman Road, anything was possible. If the intention of dumping the car at Newhaven was to throw us off the scent and cause confusion, the ploy was definitely succeeding. A lot of time and effort was going into finding not a hint that Lucan had been in the town. What was puzzling was why the length of bandaged lead pipe, the twin of the murder weapon, was left in the boot of the Ford Corsair. Lucan would know it was there and that it was an incriminating piece of evidence. He could easily have thrown it into the river to be lost in the silt, unless his mind was in such a muddle he forgot all about it. It could equally have been overlooked by somebody else driving the car who had no idea the tell-tale piece of pipe was in the boot.

I was in regular contact with Roy Ranson by telephone during the week and there was nothing moving at his end. It was agreed the following week I would travel over on the ferry to Dieppe. What I wanted to do was check exactly what the procedures were for passengers crossing to France by ferry. Though we had found Lucan's passport at his flat it was possible he had another one or he could have used a temporary 48-hour passport available at the port. If he had managed to slip aboard unnoticed he would have done one of two things: walked ashore in Dieppe or jumped overboard to certain death in mid-Channel. What I wanted to know from the experts was exactly what happened to people who leapt despairingly off ferries into the murky depths. Did they get chopped up into pieces by the powerful ship's propellers or did their bodies get carried along at the mercy of the tides and winds to be eventually washed up on the shore? I intended to find out.

11 The Eton Mafia

There was an aura of power about tycoon Jimmy Goldsmith as he sat in my office. He was a tall man with blue eyes, immaculately dressed in an expensive dark suit beneath an astrakhan overcoat. He radiated energy and the easy self-confidence I had already noticed marked out the Old Etonians. It was easy to see how he was well on his way to becoming one of the world's most successful businessmen. We wanted to speak to him because the investigation into Lucan's ailing finances had uncovered Goldsmith had arranged a loan facility for him from the Midland Bank. It took some time to set up the meeting with Goldsmith, not because he was being difficult but merely because he was rushing about all over the world tending to his complex business commitments. When he finally came into Gerald Road for an interview he was straightforward and as helpful as he could be.

Goldsmith told us some weeks before the murder Lucan had turned up out of the blue at his house in Paris and had asked for a loan of £10,000. Lucan had explained to him the problems he was having with Veronica over his children and said he thought she would part with them if he gave her enough money. Goldsmith hadn't wanted to give him a loan and generously offered him money as a gift instead. This Lucan declined, so they had settled on the loan arrangement at the Midland Bank. After Lucan departed he had never set eyes on him again.

Apart from that Goldsmith was not able to help us. I had the impression he was irritated he had become involved in the case at all. He seemed to be a man whose business success has carried him above the Clermont crowd, with the exception of John Aspinall. The two had met at Oxford through a shared interest in gambling. Aspinall had become involved in playing cards in a poker school run by Ian Maxwell-Scott, an aristocrat recklessly frittering away an inheritance. Their weekly sessions at a lodging house in Walton Street were joined by the Goldsmith brothers, first Teddy and then the younger Jimmy. It was Teddy Goldsmith, later to become one of Britain's top ecologists, who gave Aspinall his 'Aspers' nickname. Jimmy Goldsmith and Aspinall recognized in each other a common bond and the two men were to become and remain close friends. Both retained their interest in gambling, Aspinall channelling his energies into gaming clubs, Goldsmith aggressively playing roulette on a far grander scale and amassing a fortune through vast takeover battles.

At the time of our interview the involvement of Goldsmith in the Lucan saga was minimal, confined to the loan arrangement. Like others whose lives had become interwoven through a love of gambling he was to become enmeshed in the fallout from the events in the basement at 46 Lower Belgrave Street. The blows Lucan struck sent out shockwaves that were to reverberate around the world. Sir James Goldsmith, as he was to become, was one of those to whom Lucan bequeathed a painful legacy.

If Lucan had got away with his murder plot it is difficult to know if the sale of his treasured silverware would have gone ahead. He had made discreet arrangements with Christie's for the sale some months earlier when he was desperate to raise money. With Veronica out of the way there would have been no need for the sell-off. As likely as not he would have quietly withdrawn it from the auction house. Certainly selling the ancestral assets was not a decision he would have taken lightly. The silver had been in the Lucan family for generations through good times and bad. Lucan was proud of the precious collection, keeping it at the St James Club and dining off George III plates on special occasions to impress his friends.

To maintain the secrecy, Christie's catalogued the silverware as 'the property of a nobleman' and the sale could have taken place anonymously had not Veronica suspected what was happening. She had her friend Mary-Geraldine O'Donnell check on the silver and she was able to report back that part of the family crest was stamped on some of the pieces. Concerned the collection that would rightly one day belong to her son, Lord George, would be broken up and lost to the family, Veronica took legal advice from her solicitors to try and stop the sale taking place. She was unsuccessful and so, on the morning of 28 November, exactly three weeks after the murder and disappearance of Lucan, the sale went ahead just as he had arranged it except in one respect. It now took place in a blaze of press publicity.

We, too, were interested in who would turn up at the auction room and who would buy the silver. It wasn't all the Lucan silverware, but there were 102 pieces in 13 lots, most of it Georgian dinner services, plates, dishes and salvers. It had been estimated it would fetch £25,000, but by the time auctioneer Tom Milnes Gaskell brought his gavel down for the last time the total was only a disappointing £17,410. Perhaps the value of the silver had been tarnished for dealers and collectors by the Lucan affair. It wouldn't even have made that sum had not Lucan's friends been in the ring, not showing themselves personally but making bids anonymously through Christie's expert Anthony Phillips. He sat unobtrusively behind the rostrum and secured more than half of the lots for his mystery buyers. Veronica's sister Christina and her husband Bill Shand Kydd were among those who watched the proceedings in the crowded saleroom. Ostensibly they didn't buy anything, but I pondered if they had been involved in ensuring the finest Lucan silver was retained in the family where it belonged. Once Christie's had deducted their commission I wondered if they had an address for Lucan where they would send the cheque.

For a news hungry media with a hot story coverage of the hunt for Lucan was always going to be frustratingly difficult. They had a murdered nanny and a missing Earl, but linking the two too closely risked falling seriously foul of the laws governing contempt. Until he was convicted Lucan had to be considered as innocent. To say otherwise could prove expensive. The legal situation was made somewhat easier with the issue of the warrants, but newspapers still had to tread warily because what they printed was still *sub judice* in advance of a court hearing. Libel aside, the biggest problem remained the fact that Lucan's loyal band of friends were reluctant to talk to newshounds. Many of Lucan's circle were Old Etonians and I coined a phrase for them which was to catch on in print: 'The Eton Mafia'. They had an honour code which would have done the Italian mafia proud and resented any intrusion into their private world.

I, personally, didn't find them overly difficult, with one or two notable exceptions, but they had a devil-may-care attitude to authority that made them hard to interview. Social events and travel plans would be given a higher priority than tiresome police inquiries so they were frequently unavailable. When they were interviewed we usually found they were cooperative enough, but knew absolutely nothing at all that would assist us. This was widely interpreted by the press as a wall of silence erected to hamper our investigation and it was wrongly believed we were being denied crucial information. In any high profile case when there isn't a speedy arrest people start asking why not. This time the excuse was the Murder Squad was being hindered through a lack of cooperation by people in high places who had closed ranks to protect one of their own kind.

Marcus Lipton, the MP for Lambeth Central, said because of the feeling the police were not getting all the help they should in the case he would discuss it with Home Secretary Roy Jenkins. Mr Lipton said he wanted to ensure citizens were made aware that any knowledge they had of a serious crime should be given to the police. 'It looks as if some people are being a bit snooty,' remarked Mr Lipton. This widely-reported comment prompted Lucan's Old Etonian friend Charles Benson to vigorously respond in a letter published in *The Times*: 'I object to the suggestion by Marcus Lipton MP that some people are "being a bit snooty with the police" over the search for Lord Lucan. As a still close personal friend of Lord Lucan, could I make my own position clear. As far as I know, all his friends have made themselves available to the police at all times. I personally rang the department concerned on the Friday morning following the murder, giving my name and address, and also offering other names, all of whom were in full agreement. I may add that we were not contacted for some days. Is this obstruction or non-cooperation by us? Could Mr Lipton please identify those whom he believes to be failing in their public duty. If not, would he kindly withdraw his remarks.'

It was probably true enough the media hacks weren't getting very far in their approaches to the swells. Most weren't the sort of people who would even read the tabloids, let alone relish having their names splashed about in them. Brian Vine, writing in the *Daily Express*, said: 'To try to talk to this tightly knit circle of friends now is like finding a traitor in Colditz. They shrink from interview for a combination of reasons. Certainly for their heartbreak over their friend's tragedy. But more forbiddingly for fear of breaking that masonic-style bond which links that certain breed of men whose "stud book" lines mostly lead back to the same stables – privileged prep schools, Eton, Oxford, the Household Brigade. The honour code binds their silence.'

To produce their stories, feature editors had to delve deeply into their society files for background information on Lucan. This had an unfortunate consequence in that the photographs of Lucan immediately published in the newspapers and reprinted over and over again were mostly those taken on his wedding day eleven years earlier in November, 1963. These showed a boyish-looking Lucan and there were others from the same period where he looked lean and fit. The Lucan we were actually hunting already looked considerably different from this popular image of the suave charmer. A decade of drinking, smoking and eating too much rich food had turned his clean-cut jawline into puffy jowls and his hairline was showing signs of receding at the temples like that of his father and earlier Lucans. He was obviously still 6 ft 2 ins tall and hadn't lost his ramrod-straight stature, but for the public who hadn't witnessed the ageing process he could likely have avoided detection merely by shaving off his moustache or growing a beard.

In his flat we had found a photograph album of early holiday snaps of Lucan with Veronica and, loose in the book, a sheaf of others we found out were taken in Acapulco only the previous year. These more up-to-date photographs of Lucan showed how years of over indulgence had taken their toll and ravaged the heart-throb face with its finely chiselled cheekbones that had once turned women's heads. One of them was copied to show just Lucan's face for official circulation and was published in the *Police Gazette*. There wasn't any point in circulating any new photographs of a pudgy Lucan to the press because the features of slimline Lucan as he was in his carefree salad days in the 1960s were already known all over the world and the fatter version wasn't altogether different.

For hard news, journalists had to rely heavily on our regular briefings to find out what was going on. We spent time together in The Duke of Boots exchanging ideas and chatting generally. Among the regulars who shared a jar were byliners like Tom Tullet, James Fox, Owen Summers, John Penrose, Bob Traini,

Mike Fielder and Chris House, and others would call in from time to time. They had taught me the class hierarchy of readership: *Times* readers ruled the country, *Telegraph* readers thought they did, *Mail* and *Express* readers wanted to, and *Sun* readers didn't care a damn who ruled the country as long as page 3 girls had big tits.

Unlike Lucan we weren't that bothered about the way the country was being governed, except how inflation in the wake of the Middle East oil crisis was eroding our pay as prices exploded on all sides. We'd just as likely be talking about Germany beating Holland in the final of the World Cup, England not having qualified, or unsuccessful efforts going on to extradite Great Train Robber fugitive Ronnie Biggs from Brazil. If Lucan popped up in Brazil I hoped I would be the one dispatched to try and bring him back.

I was in the pub one day when two reporters from the *Daily Mail* came up to speak to me. One of them, Peter Burden, I had known for many years. We had fallen out over a story he wrote in the *Daily Sketch* some years earlier against my wishes and it had soured our relationship, the bond of trust between police officers and press being a precious commodity. The other reporter I hadn't met before. He was introduced to me as Peter Birkett.

Peter Burden said their newspaper seemed to be falling behind with the day-to-day happenings in the search for Lucan. He was getting an ear bashing from his editor, David English, who was complaining: 'I pay you a lot of money to be our top crime reporter, but you don't seem to be coming up with much information.' We had a chat and I agreed any feud we had in the past would be forgotten and we would make a fresh start. He asked me if anything was coming up that might be newsworthy. I told him about the trip I was soon to be making to Dieppe and why I was going over to France. It was agreed Peter Birkett would know the exact day I would be sailing from Newhaven on the ferry so he could follow in my footsteps and get an exclusive story. Peter Burden was pleased we had buried the hatchet and he was tickled pink his paper had the promise of a good scoop that would impress David English.

Because a gale of up to force 8 was blowing in the Channel the ferry *Captain de Gough* had not sailed from Newhaven on the night of 7 November. If it had sailed it would have been long gone before Lucan arrived. If he had decided on a ferry as his escape route to France he would have gone on the 11 a.m. sailing of the *Valencay* on Friday, so that was the ferry I used for my visit to Dieppe. There had been no sighting of him at the Newhaven port where he would have embarked, but officials were more interested in people arriving than departing. At that stage on the Friday after the murder it wasn't widely known we were looking to stop Lucan at ports, and Newhaven didn't feature in particular until the car was found.

As we had possession of his passport it was reasonable to assume Lucan would have used a 48-hour temporary passport. He had made his plans to dispose of Veronica's body, not to flee the country. Exactly how the temporary passport system worked was one of the things I wanted to check on. Basically it was a simple document, a piece of cardboard in three parts. You filled in a name and address and obtained photographs from a booth which an official at Newhaven attached to the card and stamped. Once at Dieppe a French official tore off and retained one piece and, on returning to Newhaven, the British authorities ripped off another part, leaving the traveller with a piece that explained how it all worked.

The system failed in that the French were supposed to return their section to the office at Newhaven that had issued it, thus enabling them to ensure people who left Britain duly returned before their time was up. In reality, the indifferent French often failed to do this so the system was unreliable and therefore a waste of time. People could go abroad and stay there for all time with the British authorities unaware they had gone. Similarly, people would turn up and hand in the return portion without passport control knowing they had been away and for how long. It was a lottery and Lucan could have slipped through the net, but he wouldn't have known about the loophole and it only happened to a percentage of passengers.

The journey to Dieppe took nearly four hours and gave me ample time to question the skipper and his crew on exactly what became of passengers who decided to end it all and hop over the guard rail. They said that, contrary to the popular belief that they would be sucked in and mashed to a pulp by the spinning propellers, the bodies would be tossed out, perhaps minus an arm or a leg or two. What became of them then depended on the state of the tide and prevailing wind at the time. Usually they were carried to the British coast, unless they had gone into the water close to the French side when they would fetch up there. The harbourmaster at Dieppe and his staff confirmed to me what the crew of the ferry told me about where it was known from experience bodies would float.

Where the French did score higher points for efficiency was over the fate of the bodies washed up on their beaches. I had heard back in London no determined attempt was made to identify anyone who had the misfortune to drown along the Normandy coast. The Frogs, it was said, just quietly disposed of the bodies with their typical couldn't-care-less Gaelic incompetence to avoid paperwork, and this is what could well have happened to Lucan. This wasn't the case. The French authorities assured me every inquiry was made to identify bodies. Not only that, but the authorities at Dieppe knew everything about our hunt for Lucan and had been on their toes looking out for him since the word Go. There was absolutely no way, they said, Lucan's body could have been washed up and not been identified. Another fanciful theory had gone overboard. Lucan was not buried in an unmarked grave in France.

While I was in Dieppe I took the opportunity of going on a tour of bars and cafes near the port. I was accompanied by a French CID officer who had been detailed to look after me. He knew all the likely places where someone getting off a ferry and wanting to eat without being seen would go. They were the sort of intimate establishments where an English stranger of Lucan's striking appearance would be noticed. Nobody had seen hide nor hair of him.

My investigations in Dieppe were followed closely by *Daily Mail* man Peter Birkett and provided him with lots of material for a story. On the ferry journey home he scribbled it out to ring through to his office. It was arranged with the captain he could be granted use of the ship-to-shore radio to call his copytakers and dictate the story that would be the envy of rival crime reporters. That night the printers were on strike, and the *Daily Mail* failed to appear on the street the following day.

12 Spinning Drums

I was satisfied after my detailed enquiries at both Newhaven and Dieppe that Lucan hadn't fled across the Channel on that particular ferry on the day he disappeared. It could have been, of course, that the car was dumped at Newhaven as a decoy while Lucan sailed merrily away on a ship from Dover, Folkestone or any of the other ferry ports. The ferries didn't provide the only escape route by sea on the South Coast either. There were a number of harbours like Shoreham and Chichester, packed with small boats. It would have been easy to slip away, particularly from the Hamble River further down the coast towards Southampton which wasn't policed at all. The system there relied on trust. If people didn't call up Customs and Excise and tell them they were leaving and where they were going, they would be none the wiser. I also made several trips to small airfields along the South Coast where small planes could easily take off and land with little or no control from the authorities. What my enquiries did show was just how easy it was for anyone who was determined to do so to get in and out of Britain undetected. If Lucan was still holed up in Britain and wanted to go abroad once the hue and cry died down, it would be childishly simple by either sea or air. As an expert backgammon player he would not take unnecessary risks and would be aware of the importance of knowing how far ahead he was of his opponents at all times.

The big question I had been trying to answer while I was at Newhaven was, of course, how Lucan planned to dispose of Veronica's body had his blueprint for murdering her been successful. He had intimated in his conversation with Greville Howard when he was the worse for drink that he planned to drop her body into the sea. Certainly if he had added heavy weights to the mail-bag, secured the top tightly and pitched it into a deep part of the Solent he could have watched it sink safe in the knowledge she would likely never be discovered in her watery grave. He would have had to drive to the coast and hump the mail-bag from the car boot and onto a boat at a suitable time over the weekend. This wouldn't have attracted undue attention because it was not unlike the sort of canvas sail-bag the boating crowd used and wouldn't have aroused suspicion. To be on the safe side, the boat might even have been waiting at a remote berth so his nefarious activity would not even be seen by prying eyes. But which boat and where? There were thousands of them berthed along the coast. As far as we knew Lucan didn't own a boat of his own and nobody admitted to loaning him one. He could have bought or rented one under an assumed name, or even just picked one out he had observed wasn't being used to borrow without permission and return. Many of the boats were owned by people who seldom visited them, especially out of the boating season in November. It was unlikely, but a possibility.

Without a body to bury at sea did Lucan take a boat out as he had arranged, sealing himself inside, opening the stopcocks and scuttling it to take his body instead of Veronica's to the seabed and the waiting claws of hungry crabs? I doubted it. There were no reports of any boats missing, nor reports of bits and pieces that might have floated to the surface from a sunken craft. Given the gale that was raging it would have needed expert seamanship to have put to sea on his own in darkness that night, even if the intention was to sink the boat at a chosen location. A sailing boat would have been impossible in the high wind, but Lucan would have favoured a powerboat. He knew how to handle them well from his racing days, but it would have taken all his skill not to capsize and the sound of its engine would have attracted attention in the middle of the night. Like the rest of the conjecture put forward by armchair suicide theorists, it was hard to refute because I couldn't offer a positive alternative without evidence in support.

There were those who believed Lucan flung himself bravely off a pier or simply walked into the sea and drowned. It was a popular concept at the time because of the mystery surrounding the disappearance of John Stonehouse, a former Labour government minister with business problems whose apparent drowning Miami police were suspicious about when they found his clothes on a beach but no body. On television there was a hit comedy called *The Fall and Rise of Reginald Perrin* in which actor Leonard Rossiter played a character who faked his own death in the same way to start a new life. The supposition the shamed Lucan marched boldly into the sea ignored the pounding surf on the stormy night. His body would certainly have been immediately washed back in and found, the problem with the Stonehouse bogus drowning because it raised eyebrows with those who knew how the Miami tides worked. If Lucan was serious about drowning himself why would he go to Newhaven where he might be seen rather than a deserted cove somewhere along the coast? And what would be the point of parking a distance away from the sea in a back street and walking the rest of the way to hurl himself into the surging waves? Perhaps he felt he needed to stretch his legs, get some exercise before he died.

Common sense would surely have told him a description of the car would be circulated by the police and it would soon be found. If it wasn't intended to be located quickly the car could easily have been driven off the road somewhere and hidden in woodland. That way it might have remained undiscovered for days or even weeks. The valiant peer, forever courageous in his determination to protect the family name being dragged through the courts by an ultimate act of self-sacrifice, might have done the obvious thing, launching himself off Beachy Head like many others to certain death on the rocks below. The shock of finding somebody attacking his wife had plainly inspired a burst of intelligent and philosophical letter writing. A hastily scribbled farewell note left in the car to be found after his mangled corpse would have settled his affairs and tidied the case up nicely.

It looked to me like the car had been deliberately left by somebody where it would quickly be discovered at the port. This suggested a well-contrived subterfuge to make us think Lucan had left the country so the hunt for him in Britain wouldn't be so intense. I, for one, wasn't buying any of the Newhaven business. I didn't believe he got away on the ferry to France. And I didn't think he was thinking clearly enough to improvise an elaborate method of drowning himself so his body would never be found and some honour retained for his children. Nor did I think the car had been substituted for a pile of clothes to fake drowning – it would have been left nearer the sea. Lucan hadn't given Susan Maxwell-Scott any indication he intended to kill himself. When he left her house at Uckfield he had said he must get back to sort things out. Besides which, Lucan was, above all, a gambler by nature and a gambler would see the deadly game of cat-and-mouse through to the bitter end and take his chance on not getting caught. He still held some trump cards in his hand. Could he rely on his friends to help him turn the odds in his favour?

More imaginative and even more implausible was speculation that local offshore trawlermen picked up Lucan's body in their nets, promptly sticking a boathook in it to release the air and make it sink to the bottom. There it would join others apparently littering the fishing grounds down in Davy Jones locker. According to advocates of this lurid solution, this was a well-known and frowned-on practice among fishermen to avoid a catch wasted through contamination and time-wasting red tape. If it was a regular occurrence I could find no evidence of it any more than the fable of the French callously discarding the bodies they found among the flotsam and jetsam on the foreshore. Even if it did happen occasionally, the odds on Lucan being trawled up in the vastness of the Channel to be spiked by barbaric fishermen would have run into millions, so enormous he wouldn't have placed a penny on them. But it was more grist for the Lucan rumour factory, a tasty snippet off the production line for the endless discussions taking place in spit-and-sawdust pub bars and at smart soirées as all strata of society played the popular parlour game: What happened to Lord Lucan? A hot selling line in joke shops was a lapel badge stating: LORD LUCAN. PLEASE PHONE YOUR MUMMY.

Carrying out searches of houses is known as 'spinning drums' in criminal slang. The address books we took from Lucan's flats resulted in some of the poshest 'drums' in the country being 'turned over' in the search for signs of Lucan. Ancestral piles, stately homes, country mansions, even the odd castle, were all visited by officers from forces up and down the land. It wasn't only possible Lucan could have been willingly harboured by his rich and titled friends. Such was the size of some of the properties he could have moved in without their knowledge and be hiding in the West Wing or roughing it in an empty outlying cottage on a huge estate. The owners were asked to look and check for signs of a visitor, Lucan's distinctive spoor doubtless consisting of empty vodka bottles, discarded packets of cigarettes and well-thumbed packs of cards as he whiled away empty hours in his lonely hideout playing patience. A visit from plod was a juicy tit-bit of tittle-tattle to enliven a weekend country party. Being in Lucan's little book was a sign you lived an exciting life in the fast lane with a sophisticated set of swingers and weren't the bore everyone thought.

John Aspinall's estates at Howletts and Port Lympne came under scrutiny as ideal refuges where Lucan could be concealed, totally invisible to the large staff who wouldn't notice him strolling about the paddocks among the wildlife. With Aspinall's permission policemen with dogs carried out a search of the 55-acre Howletts zoo park at Bekesbourne and the 270-acre Port Lympne estate overlooking Romney Marsh without finding anything of any significance. Word came back that when officers from the Kent Constabulary first visited Howletts they arrived during the evening and were told Aspinall couldn't see them as he was having dinner. They insisted and were led by a butler into the dining room where Aspinall was sitting with his wife and his mother at a table with a large gorilla. I hoped they checked to see Aspinall wasn't playing a joke and it was a real animal, not Lucan cunningly disguised in a gorilla skin. By then I was worried I was going as mad as everyone else.

The dragnet for Lucan spread out around the world, the FBI calling at addresses across America from New York to Los Angeles and French gendarmes knocking on doors in Paris and Frejus. The Mediterranean came in for special attention from the Sûreté National who were aiding us. Some of Lucan's wealthy friends who owned villas and apartments in the south of France could have given him a key to their vacant holiday homes. He also knew the Med well, having cruised around it with Veronica on a big yacht in their happier days in 1967, and they had stayed in Monte Carlo. In his glory days he had sped along the azure coast in his flashy power boat and it was said he was familiar with all the top casinos. It was odd how the French Riviera with its luxury villas and swish casinos was thought to be the natural habitat of a gambling dandy looking to lie low. Hidden behind sunglasses and wearing a white peaked yachting hat, it was obviously reckoned he would pass unnoticed by the Brits on the sun-kissed terraces of the best five-star hotels in Nice and Cannes. As they sipped their cognac the sozzled ex-pats would not recognize him as the man staring out from the pages of the English newspapers they were reading. The Spanish island of Ibiza, Guernsey, anywhere the rich yachting fraternity gathered, was where Lucan was frequently to be spotted, not so often working in an oily inspection pit in a garage in Milton Keynes. To be tall and dark was to easily be mistaken for Lucan. Lookalikes popped up everywhere. It even happened in the House of Lords where a visitor with a confused knowledge of history heard a speech by Lord Raglan, great-great-grandson of the one at Balaclava, and rushed up to a doorman to protest: 'He shouldn't be here. He's supposed to have murdered his nanny.'

The first published report said Lucan was heading for Haiti, his wallet stuffed full of money he had judiciously drawn out of a bank account. A telegram had arrived at his flat offering him use of a large house outside Port-au-Prince. If he had the £100,000 in readies he was rumoured to be carrying he wouldn't have been in a financial fix in the first place. Similarly, I doubted Lucan had a rumoured pile of gold Krugerrands as a hedge against the raging inflation, or a secret hoard of precious gems hidden away as easily-transported protection against a Bolshevik revolution that would require affluent right wingers to flee the country in fear of their lives. Lucan, in short, was stoney broke. Like many people with titles he was rich in assets through the family property holdings but short of hard cash, the trustees prudently only giving him a modest allowance. On the run he would have to rely on the generosity of his friends.

Millionaire Algy Cluff, a long-time friend of Lucan's from the Clermont and St James clubs, owned a house on a remote clifftop in Kent near Dover. As Windmill Cottage had an impressive wine cellar converted from a wartime bunker, it wasn't surprising we had reports that Lucan had sought refuge there. I spoke with Algy Cluff, who was the boss of an oil exploration company, and he told me he hadn't seen Lucan for about six months. I believed him, but I took the precaution of checking the wine cellar before I left.

One of the reasons I went to St Margaret's Bay myself to see Algy Cluff was that I wanted to call in and see Susan Maxwell-Scott on the way. Like Roy Ranson I wasn't happy with her account of the events at her home at Uckfield when

Lucan knocked on her door on the night of the murder. It wasn't that we thought she had committed any crime. Clearly on the basis of what she said Lucan had told her she thought he was going off to sort things out himself. In her version of his explanation he hadn't done anything wrong, nor was there any question of helping or harbouring him because there were no warrants out for him and he was merely being sought to help in our enquiries. It was what Susan Maxwell-Scott *didn't* do that bothered us.

Lucan had been with her for nearly two hours. Given the trauma of the events he had left behind, it was hardly likely they had spent much time chatting about the good old days. On the Friday she had not thought fit to mention anything about Lucan's visit, not even to her husband, and claimed she hadn't read or heard anything about the drama in which he had been involved. What she said stretched our credulity to breaking point. Roy Ranson had been to see her and she had reiterated to him what she said in her statement without adding greatly to our fund of knowledge. I thought I would try my hand and took with me DC Sally Bower.

Grants Hill House was a large Victorian building off the main road in Uckfield, a rambling ex-rectory set in a few acres. We were led into the same drawing room where Lucan had been entertained when he arrived and rang the doorbell at about 11.30 p.m. on 7 November after driving down from Belgravia. He had expected to find Ian Maxwell-Scott at home, but he was staying the night in London and his wife answered the doorbell. My understanding was Susan Maxwell-Scott let him in and poured him out a whisky and water while she herself had a coffee. According to Susan Maxwell-Scott, Lucan was wearing a pale blue polo-necked shirt with a brown sleeveless pullover, together with grey flannels which had a large wet patch on the back of the right thigh. She had not seen any blood on his clothes, nor did forensic find any on the wicker armchair he had sat on or anywhere else in the house. He could have sponged it off his flannels before he got to Uckfield, hence the damp patch, and his clothing would have been protected from the spray of blood if he was wearing the old overcoat over them at the time of the attack. But what happened to the blood-stained overcoat? We didn't find it in the dumped car at Newhaven and it hadn't been picked up anywhere along his likely routes and handed in. And how did the blood smears come to be on the envelopes posted to Bill Shand Kydd if Lucan hadn't appeared to Susan Maxwell-Scott to have blood-stains on him? It was a mystery I hoped to clear up.

Lucan told Susan Maxwell-Scott that he had been through a nightmarish experience so incredible no-one would believe it. He was right in that respect as far as I was concerned. He said he had been walking past the window of No. 46, had seen someone struggling with Veronica in the basement. This we knew from our experiments was not possible. Lucan said he had let himself into the house with his own key and the man ran off. There was blood everywhere and he had slipped and fallen into a pool of it. He had taken Veronica upstairs to wash her wounds and was then going to call a doctor and the police. While he was in the bathroom soaking towels, Veronica ran down the stairs and out of the house shouting 'Murder' and he left because the situation looked bad for him. At Grants Hill, Lucan had tried to telephone Bill Shand Kydd and had called his mother, the Dowager Countess. He had then written the letters to Bill Shand Kydd which seven-year-old Catherine Maxwell-Scott posted in the morning from the post box at the end of the road on her way to school. Susan Maxwell-Scott asked Lucan if he wanted to stay the night but he said he would get back to straighten things out and left at about 1.15 a.m. She took this to mean Lucan was going back to London and would contact the police himself. It didn't seem to occur to her that it was decidedly odd Lucan would be heading back for London when he was asking her to post letters that were going there.

I told Susan Maxwell-Scott I was concerned about what she had said in her statement, in particular her recollection of the conversation with Lucan and her description of his clothing as we thought it was likely it was covered in blood. She immediately went on the defensive, raising her voice and attacking me for doubting what she had to say. She said Lucan had not said anything relevant other than that contained in her statement and denied his clothing was blood-stained. In fact, she kept very much to what was contained in the statement so the interview and the dialogue between us did not get very far. I realized I was wasting my time asking any further questions on the conversation that had taken place between her and Lucan and the state of his clothing. She appeared to hold strong feelings about Lucan and would not go beyond what she had already said. I decided to change tack and question her about her actions on the following day. It was to be an acrimonious exchange.

I asked her: 'Did you not tell anyone about it?'

'There was no need to,' she replied. 'I was under the impression he was going back to London and would tell the authorities himself.'

'This is not something that happens to you every day of the week,' I pressed. 'A man comes to see you and tells you about this. You know him, you know his family, you share the same friends. Did you not think to tell them?'

'No.'

'Did you hear about it on the radio?'

'No.'

'But it was on the radio every half-hour, on all the bulletins. You must have heard it.'

'I don't listen to the radio.'

'It was on television. Did you see it on television?'

'No.'

'Are you saying to me none of his friends who knew about it in London telephoned you?'

'Nobody contacted me.'

'What about your husband, when did he get back home?'

'That Friday evening.'

'What did he say about it?'

'He didn't say anything about it.'

'But he had just travelled down from London. He must have known about it. It was in all the newspapers.'

'He only reads the back pages, the sports pages.'

'Didn't you get in touch with Bill Shand Kydd and ask if he had received the letters?'

'I didn't know what was in the letters.'

'Surely it didn't matter what was in the letters. The fact he wrote to his brother-in-law was enough to phone him up and ask if everything was all right. Those are the sort of questions you would expect anyone to ask.'

'Well I didn't ask any of those questions because I didn't speak to anyone. Nobody phoned me, I didn't see it on television and I didn't hear about it.'

'Are you honestly expecting me to believe what you are telling me?' I said. 'You don't listen to the radio, don't watch television, nobody contacted you, your husband didn't mention it and the first you knew about it was when one of my officers came to see you.'

'I don't care what you believe, I'm telling you what I say is the truth,' she answered.

We parted on somewhat less than harmonious terms.

13 Five Just Men

On the Friday morning following the murder there was a hastily convened luncheon meeting at the London home of John Aspinall. Present were John Aspinall himself, Bill Shand Kydd, Dominic Elwes, racing tipster Charles Benson, stockbroker Stephen Raphael, gambler Daniel Meinertzhagen, and perhaps others as well. The group who gathered at the house in Lyall Street after a quick phone-round were to become known in print as the *Five Just Men* from the Edgar Wallace book *The Four Just Men*, but clearly there were half a dozen or more people present. I wasn't sure of the names of all the people who were at Aspinall's hurriedly arranged lunch party as there were varying reports. One person who most definitely wasn't there was Jimmy Goldsmith. He was in Dublin at the time and may or may not have attended the powwow if he had been in London. In the event he wasn't present, but he was included among those named in an article in a *Sunday Times* magazine some months later that was to lead to a historical libel action with the satirical magazine *Private Eye*.

Over white wine and salad they thrashed out what was known about the sensational news that was breaking concerning their friend John Lucan. They also talked about what they might do if he suddenly turned up at their homes or called on the telephone seeking assistance and how they might be able to help him. Without much hard news of their own to go on, Dominic Elwes was dispatched to St George's Hospital to see Veronica, establish what her condition was and find out what she was saying about the melodramatic happenings at 46 Lower Belgrave Street. Elwes was emotionally upset at being told from her own mouth that it was Lucan who had attacked her. 'Now who's mad then?' she sneered. It was a good question, coming as it did from the wife of a man who had long been complaining that she was mad.

It was from Dominic Elwes we were to first hear about the summit conference of Lucan intimates in Lyall Street. He was questioned about why he wanted to visit Veronica's bedside at a time when she was still sedated. No great significance was attached to the meeting of Lucan's friends. No doubt he was the main topic of discussion at get-togethers of his cronies all over London and the phones would be ringing hot. Whatever wild and woolly ideas were put forward over the wine at the Lyall Street conflab wouldn't concern the Murder Squad unless Lucan turned up and somebody broke the law in their anxiety to help him escape justice once warrants were issued. But the meeting took on a notoriety because the people who were present wouldn't talk freely to journalists afterwards about what exactly had been discussed and decided. Not surprisingly, this was regarded with deep suspicion and a sinister rumour was spawned that Lucan's friends were conspiring to help him elude capture and smuggle him out of the country.

Dominic Elwes was quoted in the *Daily Express* as saying defensively: 'This was not an escape committee. We met as friends concerned about a man we all had the utmost affection for. Basically we discussed ways and means of helping him and his family if it became necessary.' I obviously wasn't privy to what had gone on at the meeting but, to my mind, most of Lucan's hedonistic gambling associates wouldn't be the first people I would turn to for help in organizing an escape route. It would require practical application, a different skill from picking the winner of the three-thirty at Ascot or knowing the good years for Krug champagne. They could hardly just ask the butler or the head waiter chappy to send for a cab to take Dear Johnny to Heathrow. Lucan's own lack of practical knowhow had let him down badly when he hadn't appreciated whacking somebody on the head with a lead pipe would result in a lot of mess as blood spurted out. It's not the sort of handy tip you can look up in a standard DIY manual under plumbing.

Mostly it was John Aspinall who acted as the unofficial spokesman for Lucan's coterie of friends, talking to the press and going on ITN's *News at Ten* to say: 'The case of his children, when he lost custody, was a terrible blow to him. He showed no sign of outward bleeding. The four of us who knew him best knew this caused internal haemorrhage.' Asked by the interviewer of the possibility of Lucan escaping overseas

Aspinall replied: 'I know few people less likely to be a fugitive than Lord Lucan. I find it difficult to imagine him in Brazil or Haiti.' In an interview with Peter Gladstone Smith in the *Sunday Telegraph*, Aspinall said he thought there was a fifty-fifty chance Lucan had committed suicide, commenting: 'He had honour that you could cut with a knife and if he had an inner resolve he would go through with it.'

There was a lot of talk going on about Lucan's honour and the honour code of silence being drawn around him. The aristocracy like the word, it features strongly with words like virtue and fidelity in the mottoes beneath their family coats of arms. It is a worthy quality I found hard to equate with somebody who set out to murder his wife after spreading it about she was loopy. If Lucan had a vestige of chivalry we wouldn't be looking for him because he wouldn't have tried to kill his children's mother. Having screwed it up, it would have been honourable to have kept his word and turned up at Gerald Road to face the music. There wasn't much honour to be found, either, in protecting such a man. But the upper crust concept of honour seemed to have more to do with how you behaved than what you did. It was perfectly acceptable to 'boff' a chum's wife, terribly bad form if he complained about it.

I didn't hear a lot of criticism of Lucan for murdering Sandra Rivett, only sympathy that he was on the run and praise for the restraint he had shown for so long in coping with a neurotic and shrewish wife. There was always a myth the criminal classes had their own code of honour over keeping silent, the so-called honour among thieves. This was nonsense, they would happily spill the beans about one another if it suited them. The 1960s had been the time of the super grasses, 'SG's we called them, men like Bertie Smalls and Don Barrett who sang like linnets to get reduced sentences by splitting on their mates over armed robberies. If Lucan had been from the underworld the gangsters would soon have shopped him, though some of them did have a code of honour that their womenfolk were well treated.

Four days after the murder, on 11 November, an Irish lorry driver calling himself Joe Falcon stopped Lady Sarah Gibbs in the village of Guilsborough where the Lucan children had been taken to stay at the vicarage. He told Lucan's sister he knew something about the murder and related a plausible story of how an Irish friend named Jimmy Comfort had been passing 46 Lower Belgrave Street at the appropriate time on the night of the murder when a man who was definitely not Lucan rushed out. This man bumped into him and shouted at him something like 'get out of my way' before running off into the night. As the story tied in with what Lucan had said about a 'third man' the family got excited at the prospect of finding a witness who could corroborate it. The family had further talks with Falcon and tried to track down the mystery Irishman without success. Eventually we were called in and an arrangement was made to meet Falcon at Victoria coach station in London on 23 November, but he failed to show up.

Lady Sarah had wisely taken note of Falcon's lorry firm. We were able to get hold of his address in Market Harborough from them and officers chased up the M1 to Leicestershire to interview him. He turned out to be a former professional boxer called Michael Fitzpatrick and Joe Falcon had been the name he had used in the ring. His friend, whose actual name turned out to be Jimmy Cumerford, was traced in Ireland and was able to show he wasn't in Lower Belgrave Street at the time. He said he hadn't even spoken to Fitzpatrick about Lucan. Fitzpatrick finally admitted his story was fiction, saying: 'All right. I am just a punchy fighter. I just do things out of my mind.'

For leading detectives on a wild goose chase 32-year-old Fitzpatrick was charged with wasting police time. When the case came before the Bow Street court he pleaded guilty to causing wasteful employment of Metropolitan Police officers by making a false report. The ex-boxer was fined £25 and ordered to pay £10 in costs, little enough for wasting three days of police time on useless enquiries. Presiding chairman of the magistrates Kenneth Barraclough asked him why he had made up the story. 'I cannot remember,' he replied. 'I am sorry I did it.' Mr Barraclough told him: 'Apart from wasting the time of the police you brought a lot of trouble and anguish to individual people.'

Fitzpatrick had been an amateur middleweight boxing champion who had turned professional when he was seventeen, retiring in 1971 and becoming a lorry driver. It was said in his favour he did a lot of work for charity and Sgt Forsyth told the court friends described him as a bit of a character. I was entirely satisfied it was all a piece of Irish blarney and Fitzpatrick made the story up just as he said, because he was punch-drunk from taking too many punches to the head during about 700 fights. But, as with so much else about the Lucan case, rumours persisted that it wasn't really a hoax at all and Fitzpatrick had been telling the truth. Nothing, however improbable, was being overlooked by the Lucan-is-innocent cornermen in their bid to get their man off the ropes and back in the centre of the ring where he could deliver a knock-out blow. That was unlikely, but I feared the rapscallion could get a split points decision in court if we didn't keep jabbing away at the defensive wall being erected around him.

Ian Maxwell-Scott went to the races and played poker at Oxford with John Aspinall when he would have been better occupied studying law at Balliol, losing the money left him by his late father who had been an aide-de-camp to King George V. After Oxford the two gambling friends had briefly been on-course bookies together before Maxwell-Scott dropped out after a string of losses. When Aspinall opened the Clermont Club, Maxwell-Scott went to work for him, managing the restaurant and the cellar where his extensive knowledge of wines was put to good use in establishing its reputation. Like Lucan, Maxwell-Scott suffered badly when Aspinall sold out the Clermont to Playboy with the resultant invasion by the Philistines. He came to see us at Gerald Road at my invitation so we could question him about the visit Lucan made to his house at Uckfield and what his ex-debutante wife Susan said about it. It was unfortunate he hadn't been at home when Lucan called; there might have been a different outcome to the visit if he had been there. He might even have persuaded Lucan to stay the night and accompanied him to the police station in the morning, which would have been the sensible thing to do because he hadn't helped his cause by running away.

I asked him the usual questions we were asking everyone who was being quizzed. What was his association with Lucan? When did he last see him? Where was he on the night of the murder? Then I turned to the real questions that were bothering me. Why, when he spoke to Susan on the day after the murder, was the visit of Lucan not mentioned? And how was it possible he had not read anything about the hoo-ha involving Lucan, seen it on TV, heard it on the radio or been told by friends that the police were seeking him? No, he said firmly, he hadn't known anything about the Lucan business at all that day and his visit to Grants Hill House had not been discussed with his wife.

'Mr Maxwell,' I said. 'What's the problem? You are telling me exactly the same as your wife told me. Are you seriously expecting me to believe that all that day you knew nothing about the hunt going on for Lord Lucan? For some reason you are not telling me the truth.'

'I don't like your attitude,' he said angrily.

'It's my job to investigate witnesses or people who knew Lord Lucan in an effort to establish what really happened,' I said. 'I'm sorry, but I don't believe you.'

'That's up to you,' he snapped.

As far as the investigation was concerned, there the matter with Ian Maxwell-Scott ended. He left my office to continue what struck me as a wasted and unproductive life as a compulsive gambler. I could see why Sir Andrew Clark, the eminent lawyer, had tried to prevent his marriage to his daughter Susan, reportedly saying: 'The fellow is not to my taste. He has no proper job. He is a gambler. I prefer the man who does an honest day's work to any amount of nobility or family names.' It was hard to see how anyone who was in London that day could be oblivious to the mighty uproar going on over Lucan. A person would need to be unconscious not to know about it, especially one of his best friends. Rightly or wrongly for reasons I couldn't comprehend, that is what Lucan's golfing partner Ian Maxwell-Scott was determined to maintain. It wasn't against the law to know or not know Lucan was being sought for questioning. It was just odd the great-great-grandson of Sir Walter Scott should have become so irritated when I said I didn't believe what he told me.

Ian Maxwell-Scott did tell us that when Lucan was at his house his wife had given him four sleeping tablets to swallow with a glass of water. This was an important fact she had somehow neglected to include in her original statement. With the whisky she gave him and what he might have drunk earlier in the evening the Tuinal pills could have made him drowsy and had an influence on what he did or didn't do when he left her house. Susan Maxwell-Scott was seen and confirmed it was true, saying Lucan asked if she had any sleeping pills as he might have difficulty sleeping. She said she was sorry she hadn't remembered it before, but declined to make a further statement at that time including this information. Again, a curious decision. There was nothing wrong in giving Lucan the tablets before he left.

Any gambler faced with a financial crisis would see an obvious solution: winning the money to pay off the debt. It isn't unknown for employees to take company cash for the weekend and stake it all on an even chance on the roulette wheel, black and red, odd or even numbers. They have a straight fifty-fifty chance of doubling the money, putting the firm's borrowed cash back on Monday morning with nobody the wiser, or adding the sack and a charge of theft to their troubles. As it is a do-or-die measure, the wrong prediction can result in the equivalent of the traditional leap from Suicide Rock at Monte Carlo. Watching the bouncing ball, knowing death awaits if it settles in the wrong slot, must be a terrifying experience, the ultimate gambling thrill.

Lucan would have known the answer to his problems lay on the gaming tables. A few thousand on a single number coming up on the roulette wheel would wipe out all his debts at a stroke. Like many gamblers before him, he must have been fascinated by the sweet simplicity of it and the torment of not knowing which number it would be. He borrowed heavily from his friends in the previous weeks, perhaps a lot more than we had officially been told. Not everybody told us about the money they had lent Lucan, preferring instead to just write it off. The pile of unpaid bills in his flat indicated he didn't use the money loaned to him to pay off his creditors. I guessed he used it to gamble, desperately hoping his losing streak would end and he would recover his winning touch. That would be Plan A. Only when the money had all gone down the drain did he decide to activate Plan B, the final solution, the murder of Veronica.

On further delving into Lucan's tangled finances we found he had a few thousand pounds invested in banks in Switzerland and Rhodesia. There was 20,000 Rhodesian dollars, worth about £9,000, lodged in a bank in Bulawayo, but Lucan wouldn't have been able to get his hands on it from the UK because of the foreign exchange restrictions after Rhodesia's Unilateral Declaration of Independence. At a time when Lucan invested money abroad there were restrictions on how much money could be taken out of the UK, so those people who could made arrangements to get round them. The allowance of £25 at one stage wouldn't have lasted Lucan very long in a casino on a bad night. In Ireland the Lucan family trust owned hundreds of properties in Castlebar, but the rentals being paid were extremely low, only a few pounds for each tenant. I was told the tenants, some 600 of them, had stopped paying rent when Lucan disappeared, seeing it as a golden opportunity to get some recompense for the suffering inflicted on their ancestors by the hated 3rd Earl of Lucan during the potato famine. The trust also owned a lot of land on the borders of Surrey and Middlesex, part of it potentially valuable for gravel extraction. Laleham Golf Club leased some of the land and Lucan was president and likely to remain so *in absentia*.

14 The Nob Squad

It isn't just in fictional stories that detectives attend funerals to see who turns up. There are times real detectives do it too, particularly when the funeral is for a top villain and his criminal associates can be observed paying their last respects. Crooks like flashy funerals with convoys of highly-polished black limos and extravagant flower arrangements on wooden frames, sometimes sent by the very people who killed them. Policemen also go to the funerals of murder victims, taking note of the mourners and seeing who might be slinking about among the gravestones. Such are the twisted minds of some killers that they revel in the aftermath of their crimes and get a perverted pleasure from being close by at the funerals of their victims.

We weren't expecting Lucan to be skulking about at the funeral service for Sandra Rivett held at Croydon Crematorium a week before Christmas. He wasn't a gangster or a psychopath. Crippling financial worries may have instilled demons in his head, but he wasn't a homicidal maniac. He planned to kill his wife for what seemed to him a practical enough reason: to get himself out of a financial fix and gain control of his children, not to get a depraved kick by taking her life. There was nothing to suggest he hadn't led anything but an exemplary life up to that point, nor was it likely after the gut-wrenching episode in the basement he would do anything like it in his life again. But it was an inexcusable aberration, made worse because it was coldly premeditated over a long period, and we were determined he should spend a long spell behind bars.

With Roy Ranson I attended the funeral of the murdered nanny out of respect. By one of those quirky coincidences which often happen in murder inquiries, the service took place on 18 December, Lucan's birthday. I felt sorry the life of an exuberant woman had been snuffed out like candles on a birthday cake by an emotionally-overwrought man who had dedicated his life to self-enjoyment in a twilight-zone of gaming rooms. Veronica would have attended, but it was felt her being there would result in a media circus and further distress Sandra's family. There was a report that Sandra's mother, Mrs Eunice Hensby, was already upset at Veronica because, when Sandra's aunt called to collect her clothes, they had been bundled up in paper bags and handed brusquely to her at the front door. All Veronica had said to her was: 'It's a bad business.' According to Mrs Hensby there had not been any other contact from Veronica, which surprised me because I thought she would have put pen to paper to write a letter of sympathy.

It would have been compassionate if somebody from Lucan's own family had been at the funeral. After all, it wasn't Sandra's fault she was needlessly battered to death in error. To my mind somebody on the Lucan side might have seen fit to be at the service to at least acknowledge her tragic death and be in the chapel to hear the comments of the priest. Nor did they send a floral tribute to be laid alongside those of her grieving family and close friends. There was one which said simply on the card: *To Sandra. With love from Veronica, Frances, George and Pamela*, evidently an unfortunate error by the florist for Camilla. We even sent a wreath ourselves. It was as if Lucan's family blamed Sandra for the evil that happened in the basement and the trouble poor John was in. They probably did. There were newspaper reports they had hired a private detective agency to prove Lucan's innocence should he be arrested and charged. What they would seek to substantiate was a defence that the nanny was the intended victim of an unknown assailant and Lucan the person who just happened to get involved because he was passing by the house. To have sent a representative to the funeral or even some flowers might have been construed as a gesture of apology, a tacit admission Lucan might have been responsible for her death.

These were people who, if nothing else, were well versed in the social niceties. They had a purpose in pointedly ignoring Sandra's funeral, knowing they would face inevitable criticism for appearing uncaring and heartless. Just what the private detectives would uncover was hard to see. Unlike film gumshoes, real-life inquiry agents have little scope compared to the resources we were throwing into the Lucan investigation. If we weren't able to come up with a shred of evidence to show Sandra was anything other than the unlucky victim of mistaken identity, I didn't see what anyone else could expect to find. They could only go over the same ground and speak to the same people. This would tell them it was Sandra and not stressed-out Lucan who was deserving of sympathy. As her coffin disappeared behind the curtain, I wondered where Lucan was celebrating his fortieth birthday, a milestone Sandra would never see.

In America the fallout from the burglary at the Watergate Building in Washington was still making big news. Richard Nixon, the first US president to resign from office, was granted a full pardon by his successor Gerald Ford but there was a lot of speculation going on about a cover-up and abuse of power by the President's Men. While that was happening, I was involved in an investigation with Roy Ranson that threatened to blow up into Britain's answer to Watergate, a mysterious break-in and theft of papers belonging to Prime Minister Harold Wilson. Lucan was taking up the majority of my time, especially in the early stages, but it wasn't all that was happening at Gerald Road and normal CID matters still had to be investigated and, hopefully, cleared up. When the papers were stolen in October there were suspicions voiced by Harold Wilson that it was part of a sinister plot by right wingers to discredit him by suggesting he had links with the Soviets. It was even said the British Secret Intelligence Service, MI5, was behind the burglary and that they were bugging his conversations in a bid to get damaging evidence against him as part of a right wing 'dirty tricks' smear campaign involving the Americans and South Africans.

During lengthy inquiries I visited No. 10 Downing Street a number of times and got to know Harold Wilson fairly well. I liked him. He didn't laugh a lot, but he had a dry wit. He demonstrated it when I was at his office one day on the morning after he had been in the House of Commons. 'Huh, I had a right day yesterday at Question Time,' he said with a straight face. 'What do you think? The Hon Member for Nottingham got up and asked what I did yesterday? I said, apart from other things, I visited Nottingham and opened a civic centre. Then I sat down. The Hon Member got up again and asked if I would be good enough to tell the House why, when I visited Nottingham to open the centre, I failed to visit the polluted River Trent. I stood up and I said I was asked what I did yesterday, not what I didn't do.' He still kept a straight face.

On the day after Sandra Rivett's funeral, I went to see a wealthy property developer named Eric Miller. The Prime Minister's papers had been stolen from an office at 21 Buckingham Palace Road owned by Miller, who was chairman of the Peachey Property Corporation and was also chairman of Fulham Football Club. He was a supporter of Harold Wilson and was happy to store some of his personal tax papers at the office when he had moved out of No. 10 after his first stint as Prime Minister. It was necessary to see Miller several times to try and get to the bottom of who might have been behind the theft. He was a high flyer and offered the use of his helicopter if it would help in the search for Lucan, which was public-spirited of him but wouldn't have helped. It was clear from what he told me that the theft of the PM's papers was a straightforward criminal act by people who wrongly thought they could pick up some money from them.

Exactly a year to the day after Sandra's funeral, again on Lucan's birthday, I went with Roy Ranson for a clandestine meeting with an informant at the Holiday Inn in North London. As a result we recovered a box containing the papers stolen in the raid. Arrests were made and a number of people were convicted for burglary and/or receiving stolen property. If the MI5 'spooks' had been involved, the missing papers would likely have mysteriously turned up somewhere on a rubbish tip and a lowly clerk blamed for being careless. That was the way they operated. Harold Wilson wasn't correct in thinking MI5 had a hand in stealing his tax papers, but he was probably right in thinking they were checking up on him because of suspicions of a pro-Soviet cell at No. 10 resulting from his trips to Moscow.

During our inquiries into the stolen papers we recovered, it was necessary to take elimination fingerprints from those people on Wilson's staff who had legitimate access to them, a laborious but necessary task for the forensic experts. These included Marcia Williams, later to become Lady Falkender, a much-feared woman who ran Wilson's so-called Kitchen Cabinet at No. 10. We had great difficulty getting her to give her fingerprints. Appointments would be made and broken. Such was the extraordinary power she wielded we knew there wasn't any point in appealing to Wilson. He would only have put his hands in the air and said: 'Look, I'm only the Prime Minister.' Coupled with the fact Marcia Williams had refused to be positively vetted we became suspicious she had a skeleton in her cupboard, some dark secret from her past she didn't want us to know about because her prints were on record somewhere. Eventually an appointment was made and wasn't broken and her fingerprints were taken, Wilson wandered in at that exact moment in shirt sleeves and braces, just as if somebody had pulled a cord. 'Oh, you've finally got her fingerprints, then?' he said. The fingerprints were run through the files and didn't match up with any in the records.

It was Lady Falkender who was credited with putting together Harold Wilson's notorious honours list when he resigned as Prime Minister for no reason that I could ever fathom. It became known as the 'Lavender List' because it was said a draft had been originally scribbled out in her handwriting on her personal notepaper. Among those honoured with a knighthood was Eric Miller, who shot himself the following year when his property empire collapsed and he faced the prospect of appearing in court for fraud. There were peerages for Wilson's raincoat manufacturer, Sir Joseph Kagan, his publisher, Sir George Weidenfeld, and another property man, Sir Max Rayne, as well as knighthoods for impresarios Bernard Delfont and Lew Grade. The capitalist make-up of the honours enraged Labour MPs, more than 100 of them publicly disassociating themselves, and Tory Members joked that there had not been an honour for Wilson's labrador dog Paddy. Kagan later had his knighthood taken away when he was jailed for fraud, Wilson having to deny he had access to classified information when it was known he was friendly with a fellow Lithuanian who was a KGB officer at the Soviet Embassy.

On the controversial honours list was the name of international financier Jimmy Goldsmith, known to be a cash supporter of the Conservatives so not a popular figure with Labour. He received a knighthood 'for services to exports and ecology', which was thought to be odd by my press friends because as chairman of Cavenham Foods he was not a serious exporter. Nor was he a recognized ecologist – that was his brother Teddy. Goldsmith's name was on a list leaked to the press in advance as destined for a peerage, featuring in a famous *Daily Express* headline: IT'S LORD GOLDSMITH. The peerage was seemingly queried and reduced to a knighthood by the scrutiny committee after intervention by the Queen or new premier James Callaghan.

Sir James Goldsmith was said to be disappointed he did not get a peerage. He had designs on becoming a press baron as a Lord and coveted a political role in government. It didn't happen. The curse of Lucan was to involve him in a legal battle with the scurrilous magazine *Private Eye* that dragged on from January, 1976, to May, 1977, and damaged his reputation. It was one thing to make it crystal clear he did not play a part in any conspiracy that might have been suggested over Lucan, uncharacteristically ill-judged to go way over the top and make himself unpopular by firing a fusillade of writs and suing *Private Eye* for criminal libel into the bargain. The 'Lavender List' probably dashed Wilson's own retirement aspirations as well. He was passed over for a mastership of both University College, Oxford, and Trinity College, Cambridge.

On most major murder inquiries a tie is struck to mark the event as a keepsake, usually designed by somebody manning the phones on the late shift bored after reading the papers and doing the crosswords. If the design is approved by senior officers it is reproduced by one of the many specialist shops. The tie for the Lucan case was unusually tasteful, a small coronet over the initial L which looked particularly stylish in gold on a blue tie or the corner of a silk headscarf for women officers or wives and girlfriends. They became best sellers and were a popular Christmas gift. The ties were worn with pride. There was kudos attached to working on the Lucan team. It went to the head of one young detective who had to be transferred to other duties after he had too much to drink in the bar at the Clermont one night and got into a barney with the manager.

Not long after the inquiry started a name was coined for the Lucan murder squad: the 'Nob Squad'. Given our failure to turn up the erring earl, it was inevitable the Nob Squad would come in for a good deal of criticism, some of it justified, some not. The image of flatfooted Inspector Plod of the Yard blundering about, notebook in hand, in the drawing rooms of country houses wearing a trilby hat and trenchcoat was a familiar one from numerous stage plays and movies. We were said to be out of our depth in an unaccustomed social milieu, taunted by people who mocked us mercilessly and had great fun playing jolly jokes at our expense. It wasn't true we weren't used to dealing with upper class people. After all, we worked among them all the time in Belgravia. We basically knew how to raise our little pinky as we drank tea from bone china cups and we didn't hold classes to tell squad members the correct forms of address and not to spit on the carpet. But some of our cousins from other forces may have been embarrassed asking to search the dusty attics of mansions for Lucan.

Where we perhaps did defer too much was in not treating the titled and ultra-rich like everyone else when we wanted to interview them. In the East End we would not have hesitated in knocking on doors of people we wanted to see in the middle of the night, kicking down the flimsy doors of high-rise flats if they were suspected of wrongdoing. This didn't happen in the Lucan case, especially if the person behind the iron-studded door of a castellated country house might well sit on the police authority or be a local magistrate. Mostly we had to make appointments, and these were not always treated with the urgency and gravitas required. The interview with Ian Maxwell-Scott was a case in point. He came to see us only after we finally insisted and was plainly irritated when he arrived, so we got off on the wrong foot in a hostile atmosphere.

There were suggestions People-In-High-Places didn't actually want Lucan to be caught at all and so quietly brought pressure to bear for us to go easy and come up empty handed. This was nonsense. It was just the opposite: a high-profile case with pressure on to get a result. Everything that could be done was done and everyone on the force would have been delighted to see the handcuffs on Lucan. To his gambling friends Lucan was a charming and tolerant man whose patience with his quarrelsome wife finally snapped, an understandable infringement that could happen to any red-blooded male. In their eyes he merely tried to kill his wife, something troublesome spouses might expect if they behaved badly. It showed a lack of emotional control and he botched it up, but it wasn't as if he did anything really terrible, like voting Labour. To us Lucan was just a man wanted for a particularly nasty murder, the fact he killed Sandra Rivett and and not Veronica was of no consequence in our determination he should pay the price. I suspected most of the aristocracy who didn't know Lucan personally would also welcome seeing him pay his debt to society. The feckless manner in which he trifled away his life gambling wasn't how they liked to portray themselves as hard-working and responsible citizens putting their fortunes to good use.

The other criticism was the cost of the operation. Obviously it was expensive, though not horrendously so for the Metropolitan Police when compared to the bills for dealing with large-scale public disorders involving busloads of uniformed officers. In 1974 murders were regarded as special inquiries, and this meant all the work was done on overtime, so it was a nice little earner for those on the squad. There was no way of calculating the total cost of the whole exercise because it involved inquiries being carried out by forces throughout Britain and all over the world. All the police officers involved would have been working anyway. The cost was academic in that it only meant allocating their time to Lucan rather than anything else. If he had been picked up in the first few days there wouldn't have been much expenditure involved. It mounted up because he escaped capture and nobody knew where he was as the weeks dragged on.

15 Caught in the Spider's Web

In every chain there is one weak link waiting to break at any time and cause chaos. Within Lucan's ring of cohorts that link was Dominic Elwes. The son of portrait painter Simon Elwes, Dominic was a Catholic so didn't attend Eton like most of the others, going instead to Downside and somehow getting himself expelled. After a brief spell in the army he gained something of a reputation as a society bounder and playboy in the 1950s, culminating in his much-publicized elopement in 1958 with heiress Tessa Kennedy, their marriage in Cuba ending in divorce eleven years later. Elwes never seemed to settle down to any steady job, painting the odd portrait, but usually short of funds and relying heavily on the generosity of his rich friends. He repaid them by making them laugh. His easy charm and natural gift as a raconteur with a string of entertaining anecdotes made him agreeable company, able to set a table on a roar. His world as a *bon viveur* revolved around the Clermont and Annabel's, where he paid for his supper with his ready wit. To me there was a darker side to Elwes, the hidden face of the clown who makes people laugh while suffering personal angst. When I met him he always appeared to be a sensitive soul with a nervous disposition. I could see how he drew emotional support as well as the wherewithal from his soul-mates at the Clermont. There were stories that Elwes had been an adventurer in his younger days, battling bravely with the partisans against Russian tanks in Hungary in 1956. He was said to have passed military secrets to Colonel – later Sir – David Stirling, legendary creator of the 1st Special Air Service Regiment, the SAS, in North Africa in World War Two, and who was involved in the Yemen in the 1960s on behalf of the Royalists.

When I was lecturing at the CID school in 1970 one of the subjects missing was the art of interrogation. Everyone had thought since time immemorial it was something you couldn't teach. You learned it as part of your apprenticeship and got better with practice. Somebody said the Army ran interrogation courses and I ought to have a look at it so I got permission to go down to the Intelligence Corps at Templer Barracks, Ashford, as an observer for two weeks. The courses were being held because the likes of Colonel Stirling had trouble in Aden questioning tribesmen to get information for their guerrilla operations. It was an excellent course involving the use of sensory deprivation like white music and the video recordings of interviews. A lot of the course was adapted and used in the syllabus for CID training.

In the evenings I spoke to the instructors in the officer's mess and they told me, as far as they were concerned, there would soon be political killings in Britain. It was a novel notion because there hadn't been any up until then and, on my return, I spoke to Vic Gilbert, the Commander of Special Branch, about it. He didn't agree completely, but I could see Special Branch were working along the same track, as were the branches of the secret services. Colonel Stirling retired in 1973 and the following year formed the Greater Britain league, seeing a takeover of the Labour Party by left-wing activists as posing the most menacing crisis the country had ever faced, more dangerous even than the worst period of World War Two. His ideas were scoffed at by most of the press as 'Colonel Blimp' nonsense, but the unions were riding high and his fears hit the right note with Lucan's crowd. So concerned was Lucan about the state of the nation, John Aspinall revealed he was about to make his maiden speech in the House of Lords on immigration at the time he disappeared. I don't know how true it was. The Red Army would need to be marching up The Mall before the gamblers at the Clermont would drag themselves away from the gaming tables. Elwes didn't strike me as a man of action, either, and it may have been romantic fantasy he fought the Russians. I was in an *Alice in Wonderland* world where nothing was what it seemed to be.

One day Elwes came to see me at Gerald Road. I was out at the time, but hurried back because I thought he might have some important information to impart. He said he was concerned about a bunch of parking tickets he had accumulated, saying he believed the police were hounding him and he was worried he would go to prison for non-payment of fines. I pointed out that if he made some offer to pay the fines off it was highly unlikely he would be jailed, but it was hard to pacify him. The parking tickets were a trivial matter. It wasn't unknown for residents in Belgravia to ignore parking restrictions, return a pile of tickets with a note with 'Bollocks' scrawled on it, and leave it for doting parents or indulgent trustees to sort out. I wondered if there was an ulterior and more serious purpose to the visit of Elwes and his obvious distress.

Elwes was the man sent from the Aspinall lunch to Veronica's hospital bedside to find out what it was she was intending to say about Lucan's attack on her, breaking down in tears when she said she was naming her husband as the man who tried to kill her. Were the parking tickets just an excuse to see me? Was it another fishing expedition, an opportunity to gauge the situation from my attitude because he feared he was exposed to something more threatening to his freedom than parking fines? I suspected someone other than Lucan dumped the Ford Corsair at Newhaven, or at least was with him when he did it to drive him away. It could have been Elwes; that would account for why he was so edgy. Something was worrying him a lot to make him so nervy. Did he know more than he was letting on about the disappearance of Lucan? The fact the parking fines were unpaid indicated he was hard up, but that probably wasn't an unusual state for him to be in. I doubted that he would have that much fear of prison. He had spent a couple of weeks inside purging his contempt of a High Court injunction over his elopement with Tessa Kennedy. There had to be something else preying on his mind.

An amusing cartoon by Keith Waite in the *Daily Mirror* depicted two Australian policemen on camels in the outback asking an aboriginal cooking a lizard over a fire: 'Lord Lucan?' Down Under in the antipodes was one of the places where Lucan was supposed to have gone to earth. In December police in Melbourne thought they had hit the jackpot when they picked up a cultured Englishman who closely answered his description. It turned out to be not Lucan but John Stonehouse, the former Labour MP and Postmaster General who had supposedly drowned in the sea off Miami. He arrived in Australia on a false passport, aiming to start a new life as British police investigated his involvement as chairman of a crashed Bangladesh bank. He might have got away with it if he hadn't borne a passing resemblance to Lucan and stood out for being distinguished among the Aussies. That, and Oscar winner Glenda Jackson's TV appearance as Cleopatra on the *Morecambe and Wise Show*, gave us the biggest laughs over Christmas. Red-faced Australian police were determined not to get caught out a second time and asked us to send over more details of Lucan. We did and they picked up another man, a boilermaker from Blackmore in Essex named Kenneth Knight. Australia was in the news again over Christmas, a cyclone called Tracy destroying the city of Darwin. Perhaps it was just Lucan hitting town and causing more devastation.

After the Christmas holiday a decision was taken to run down the murder squad. The trail was going cold and it was obvious that, wherever he was, he wasn't actually going to be found. The high power of the early days of the inquiry had fizzled out, so it was logical to reduce the number of people employed on the case.

Sgt John Hefford was kept on as office manager and he retained several detectives to continue with the investigation. By then, a great deal of the routine work had been completed with many hundreds of statements taken and on file. There was still plenty to keep the smaller team busy, but the rest went back to other duties, disappointed at our failure to find the errant earl. As long as Lucan remained at liberty, or until his body was discovered, the case would never be closed. Years later the dockets would still be kept, with fresh statements and exhibits added as new information came to light. Lucan would never again be able to sleep easy. He would always be expecting the tap on the shoulder that would tell him the long arm of the law had caught up with him.

There wasn't much more that could be done that wasn't already in hand, so our thoughts turned to the inquest on Sandra Rivett. This had been briefly opened by the Coroner of Inner West London, Dr Gavin Thurston, and adjourned after evidence of identification in the expectation that Lucan would be arrested. When this didn't happen by the New Year, meetings were held with Dr Thurston about a date for the resumed inquest and with representatives from the office of the Director of Public Prosecutions, Sir Norman Skelhorne, about

Caught in the Spider's Web

people we had interviewed who could be called and statements that could be presented. Dr Thurston would have to decide the list of runners and riders for the hearing and what evidence the jury would be permitted to hear. It was obvious, whether he liked it or not, the inquest was inevitably going to become a murder show trial with worldwide interest centred on it.

It wouldn't be the first time Dr Thurston had conducted inquests in the full glare of the media spotlight. During his long career he had handled inquiries into the deaths of celebrities like Judy Garland and Jimi Hendrix. He was going to have a difficult task on his hands with Sandra Rivett and would need all his skill to keep the hearing on track within the confines of what it was supposed to accomplish, and not let it turn into a public post-mortem on the entrails of the Lucans' marriage. The main problem was what Veronica would say. In law a woman could give evidence against her husband for an assault on her, but not on other matters. While she had told me Lucan had confessed to killing Sandra as they sat exhausted on the stairs, it was not something she could go on a witness stand and say as a prosecution witness.

Ostensibly the inquest would look into how, where and by what means Sandra Rivett met her death. It wasn't about the attack on Veronica. Deciding how Sandra died would be easy enough; the ticklish bit would come next. It would be for the jury to decide who might be charged with murder or manslaughter as a consequence of her death. As the law stood at the time, Lucan would, to all intents and purposes, be on trial for murder because Veronica would duly name him as her attacker and the jury would have to make up their minds if he was also responsible for the nanny's death. Lucan wouldn't be there in the coroner's court to defend himself. Nor would evidence be put forward on his behalf or pleas made by a lawyer because that wasn't the purpose of the inquiry. If Lucan didn't want that to happen, he could, of course, give himself up and try and persuade a jury in a criminal court he was innocent of the murder of Sandra Rivett. Then a jury would at least hear what he had to say and he would get a fair crack of the legal whip. The fact Lucan would effectively be tried at the inquest was causing press comments and consternation in legal circles over the incongruity of the ancient rules governing inquests. Coroners' courts were among the oldest in the land, the office dating back well over a thousand years. Clearly the rules were unfair and in need of updating. There was also a lively debate going on over whether Lucan could even be guaranteed a fair trial in a criminal court because so much had already been written about him in the papers. Anyone sitting on a jury would certainly have read a good deal about the case. It had become almost a national obsession. The *New Law Journal* said publicity had already prejudiced the issue and finding an unbiased jury would be extremely difficult at the very least.

For some time after the murder Veronica maintained a dignified silence about the events of the night of 7 November, getting increasingly annoyed at the wild rumours that always seemed to paint her in a poor light and present her husband as a paragon of virtue. She finally decided to enter the fray and fight back with an exclusive interview splashed in the *Daily Express* on 20 January. It was written by Brian Vine and Owen Summers and described in great detail how she fought a battle of desperate ferocity for her life while the body of the murdered nanny lay near by. The story was carefully worded so as not to actually identify the intruder by name for legal reasons, but only the thickest of readers would not know who it was she was talking about. Not only did she go into a blow-by-blow account of the attack on her, she staged a step-by-step reconstruction for photographer Harry Dempster. In one picture Veronica was standing on the exact spot in the basement where the body of Sandra Rivett was found near the piano, with a photograph on the wall above of Lucan in a group with other boys at Eton. I knew how difficult it had been for Veronica to continue living in the house after the attempt on her life. It must have been an ordeal to relive the nightmare to defend her name against her detractors.

There wasn't anything new in the story as far as I was concerned. It was largely a repeat of what she said in her original statement and what I had talked over with her on a number of occasions, sometimes in The Duke of Boots when it was quiet and I knew the press gang wouldn't be there. She had told me herself how Lucan had rushed out of the cloakroom and hit her on the head and tried to choke her by thrusting his gloved fingers down her throat before trying to strangle her. It wasn't news to me how she had fought him off and had pretended she would help him do something about Sandra Rivett's body, but it was a startling revelation to the great British public. What the *Express* story did do was cast Veronica in a new and sympathetic light, a deep three-column photograph on the front page showing her in ribbed jumper and tweed skirt fondly cuddling Sandra Rivett's black cat Tara on her lap. Another showed her sitting waif-like in an armchair looking enigmatically at a portrait of Lucan by Dominic Elwes propped up against the fireplace waiting to be hung on the wall alongside his illustrious ancestors. I had smiled at Lucan's wry humour in hanging pictures of the 3rd Earl of Lucan and his brother-in-law Lord Cardigan on opposite sides of the dining room, glaring accusingly at one another over responsibility for the balls-up at Balaclava.

Somewhat surprisingly in the circumstances, Veronica also spoke compassionately of the husband who wished her at the bottom of Seven Mile Deep in the Solent. She said he was a tragic person with talent and enthusiasm who would have been successful in any other profession if he had not chosen the life of a gambler and she felt sorry for him. Veronica idolized Lucan at the time they were married, blind to the fact he was an inveterate gambler and gave not the slightest indication he would give up what he regarded as his job. It was apparent she still had strong feelings for the man she had once worshipped, despite the way he had treated her and what had happened. She seemed to think Lucan had been influenced by others, realizing he had done the wrong thing in leaving her and coming to value the stability of a home background and children. I wondered how far, if we caught Lucan, she would go in ensuring his conviction and imprisonment or whether she would end up feeling sorry for him and plead on his behalf for leniency.

In the interview Veronica seemed to be speaking more in sorrow than anger. Her warm comments about Lucan must have come as a surprise to many people who were gossiping on the Mayfair dinner circuit. This surely wasn't the harpy of popular myth whose sharp-tongued vindictiveness had finally driven her long-suffering husband over the abyss. Here was a woman who had undergone a terrible ordeal and yet was still prepared to speak in affectionate terms of the estranged husband who wanted her dead. The family of Lucan must have hated the article. It strongly suggested without actually saying it that

Lucan was the man Veronica was referring to as the unnamed intruder. Nor did she come across as being the mentally unbalanced harridan she was supposed to be. Veronica wasn't hugely critical of anyone in particular but, describing the break-up of the marriage, she said they had been surrounded by jealous, bickering people who just couldn't stop putting the knife in and that pulled them apart.

In the early hours of Monday, 26 January, Susan Maxwell-Scott got in touch with the *Daily Mail* and told them she had received a call on the phone from Post Office Telegrams to say Lucan was safe and well. She had written down the cryptic message and it said: TELL MOTHER ALL WENT AS PLANNED. I AM SAFE HERE. LOVE JOHN. The first we knew about it was when it appeared in the newspaper and it wasn't mentioned to the police by her husband until 12.50 p.m. that day. Given her strange behaviour in the past this didn't come as the surprise it might have done, though why she should choose to tell a newspaper first and not the police was anyone's guess. When she was interviewed about the telegram her story was she thought it was a cruel hoax. So why had she told the *Daily Mail* about it, knowing it would result in a lot of publicity? Certainly the telegram seemed to be a hoax on somebody's part. The General Post Office ran a check and failed to trace the telegram through the Brighton office which would have handled it or the woman clerk supposed to have rung it through to Uckfield. But who was responsible for the hoax and why? At this interview Susan Maxwell-Scott at least agreed to make a statement in which she said she had given the four tablets to Lucan before he left her house never to be seen again. In his official report Roy Ranson wrote that he had been led to believe Susan Maxwell-Scott had an infatuation for Lucan and that might well have been the reason for her reluctance to tell the whole truth. Certainly her behaviour all along was curious. She struck me when I met her as a highly intelligent woman and I could see no logical reason why she hadn't gone straight to the police on every occasion and told them everything she knew.

Bankruptcy proceedings were started against Lucan on 29 January by two firms who said he owed them £1,500 over his Mercedes-Benz car, outstanding from a hire purchase agreement and unpaid repair bills. The two companies, H.W. Motors and Bowater Securities, of Walton-on-Thames, Surrey, filed their petition in the London Bankruptcy Court. Through their solicitors they maintained Lucan departed out of England or departed from his dwelling house or otherwise absented himself in order to defeat or delay his creditors, supporting their contention with newspaper clippings. I thought it unlikely Lucan fled to defeat or delay his creditors. Evidently I was labouring under a misapprehension in thinking his main motivation was that he didn't want to fall into our hands. What Lucan said he feared would happen in his conversation with Greville Howard *had* happened: the family name had been dragged into the bankruptcy court. Greville Howard had counselled him that it would be better to be in court for bankruptcy than murder. He had ignored the good advice and faced the prospect of ending up in both. Dennis Gilson, the accountant who was the trustee for the creditors, dug deeply into Lucan's family treasure chest and eventually raised £118,000 from his estate and paid off all the creditors. Four trunks full of silver which once belonged to the 3rd Earl were found in the vaults of Lloyds Bank, including a large candelabrum topped by a hideous skull and crossbones. The silver was sold off at auction on 31 March 1976, together with his coronet, his Coronation robes and his much-loved pair of shotguns. It was an act to set Lucan's ancestors spinning like tops in their graves.

On the day of Sandra Rivett's funeral, before going to Croydon Crematorium for the service, I met with solicitors at Lucan's flat in Elizabeth Street to discuss with them the removal of his personal possessions. The agents for Grosvenor Estates wanted to repossess the flat and have it cleaned up so it could be let to a new tenant. Arrangements were made for his effects to be given to Veronica at the house in Lower Belgrave Street: his well-tailored suits, personal knick-knacks and the photo album with the snaps taken in Acapulco. Returned to her also was the large oil painting by Dominic Elwes which was shown in the *Daily Express*. It depicted a gloomy looking Lucan in his scarlet robe with its ermine collar silhouetted ominously against a stormy sky.

16   The Gorilla Man

It may or may not have been true that Lucan confided in John Aspinall's mother, Lady O, that he intended to kill Veronica and she told him to do whatever he thought was right. There were plenty of stories about Lady Osborne going the rounds. She was a strong character with a sharp wit who I heard described from the days when she was involved in her son's floating chemmy games as 'Al Capone with a shopping basket' or 'the Mafia with a handbag'. When the police raided Aspinall's gambling party at her flat in Hyde Park Street and arrested them for running a common gaming house she reportedly said to the officer: 'Young man, there was nothing common here before you walked in.' During the early days of the hunt for Lucan she was said to have ended a telephone conversation by saying: 'Sorry, must go. Got to go and give Lucky his food. He's down under the tiger cage.'

The doughty Lady O acquired her title following her second marriage to George Osborne, heir to a baronetcy dating from 1639. Born in India, where her family had long lived and worked, she was named Mary Horn but was known as 'Polly'. Her marriage to a medical officer in the Indian Army ended in divorce and she took her two children to England. According to Brian Masters in his biography *The Passion of John Aspinall*, he grew up believing Colonel Robert Aspinall was his father. But when he went to him for a loan to pay off debts picked up at Oxford, he was told he couldn't have the money. Colonel Aspinall said he had paid for his education and would give no more as he was not his real father. He gave Aspinall £5 for the train fare to his home at Framfield near Uckfield. It struck me as odd that both Aspinall and Lucan, when faced with a crisis resulting from debts, had headed for Uckfield.

The admission from his mother that his actual father had

been a captain in the Lincolnshire Regiment did not disappoint Aspinall. George McIlree Bruce was a World War One hero who was born in Canada of Scottish ancestry which could be traced back to Scandinavian origins and explained his fair appearance. Aspinall traced him through the army lists. By then he was a retired major-general. Always a good story-teller, Aspinall liked to tell the tale of what happened when he rang the doorbell of his flat in Camden Hill Gardens and announced: 'I'm your son.' His father looked at him and said: 'You're Polly's boy, aren't you? This calls for a celebration.' He opened a whisky bottle and the two were to become good friends.

Aspinall is a great believer in the lineage of inherited genes, both for humans and animals, resulting in a natural hierarchy in which the strong provide for the weak. His élitist view of an aristocracy of people congenitally suited to be leaders struck a chord with the Clermont set. Some, like Lucan, saw themselves as a race apart, a different species from the common herd because of their breeding. It wasn't surprising we came across tapes of Hitler's speeches in Lucan's flat. He certainly was a man with strong ideas on eugenically improving the German race by selection.

When the chips were down and Lucan needed a friend it was only Aspinall who publicly came right out and said he would have helped Lucan had he been asked to do so. In his eyes the measure of true friendship was helping a friend when things were going badly and they were in trouble, not when everything was fine. He was quoted as saying: 'If a close friend of yours came in covered in blood, having done some frightful deed, the last thing that would have occurred to you is to turn him in. It goes against every last instinct of human loyalties, and to hell with the law or the common norms of civic behaviour or something. If he had begged asylum he would have had it. I would have helped him. If he had turned up at Howletts, I would have taken him aside and had a long talk and looked at the problem. It may have involved him giving himself up or getting him funds to go to Costa Rica. He could certainly have had a lot of money. I had many people calling me and saying, if Lucan wants money, he can have it.'

When I read what Aspinall said I thought at least he had the courage of his convictions, a loyal friend who Lucan could have relied on had he chosen to ask him for help. Aspinall also seemed to sympathize with Lucan over his attempt to batter his wife to death, reportedly telling the police officers who interviewed him: 'If she'd been my wife, I'd have bashed her to death five years before and so would you. Who knows into what red hell one's soul will stray under the pressure of a long, dripping attrition of a woman who's always out to reduce you, to whom you are stuck and from whom you've had children.' On television Aspinall was interviewed by Ludovic Kennedy and asked what he would do if Lucan walked into the room. 'I would embrace him,' he replied without hesitation.

Aspinall's loyalty to his friends was extended to the gorillas and tigers he bred at Howletts, lavishing attention on them and freely romping in their cages. It was a trust not always repaid by the animals. In 1970 a pregnant tiger named Zorra attacked 12-year-old Robin Birley, the son of Lady Annabel and Mark Birley, gripping his head in its mouth and crushing his face. Aspinall prised the tiger's jaws apart and the boy was rushed to hospital five miles away in Canterbury where doctors saved his life. Aspinall's faith in the relationship between man and beast suffered other setbacks, too, with the deaths of three keepers, two mauled by a tiger Aspinall then shot, the third crushed by an elephant against a fence. His typically unconventional methods of establishing breeding colonies of increasingly rare tigers and gorillas by treating them with more respect and comfort than other zoos nonetheless brought success and earned him worldwide recognition as a conservationist.

With the coming of spring the focus again centred on the South Coast. Holiday flats, chalets and caravans would be opening up again, and people would be visiting the boats that had been tied up for the winter. The police forces in Hampshire, Sussex and Kent were asked to get in touch with their local media to ask for the co-operation of the public so hikers would be on the lookout. Nothing was uncovered. The empty holiday properties revealed no decayed body of Lucan, nor was he found mouldering among the hedgerows by strolling groups of happy ramblers. All along the coast owners returned to their yachts and motorboats without discovering his body below decks, nor signs he might have camped in one. If Lucan had owned a boat himself it would have been discovered. There were few places where it could have been moored without having to pay dues.

On 16 May I was back in Newhaven myself to meet Home Office officers from the Police Development and Research Branch and scientists from the Radar Centre at Havant. The boffins from the Plessey electronics group had come up with a revolutionary piece of equipment that would assist in the search. It was a small one-man autogyro fitted with ultra-violet and infra-red cameras that could take X-ray photographs. The idea was the little aircraft would fly low over about six-square-miles of downland behind Newhaven taking photographs, and these would miraculously show bodies buried in the ground beneath the dense gorse. It was claimed the equipment was so sensitive the cameras could detect bodies of even small animals buried up to 3 ft deep with the autogyro flying at a height of up to 2,000 ft. I was sceptical, if only because I was uncertain how Lucan would have managed to bury himself.

The autogyro turned out to be a magnificent piece of flying machinery, worthy of Heath Robinson at his best. The intrepid pilot, Wing Commander Kenneth Wallis, was precariously perched on the front of a metal framework pushed noisily along by a petrol-powered propeller while the rotor blades whirled dangerously close to his helmet. He was a former bomber pilot and had built the machine himself. The press photographers loved it and the flying eye-in-the-sky made excellent copy, especially when the brave Winco had to make an emergency landing. It was a spectacular performance, spoiled only by the fact it didn't work. The composite multi-band picture built up from more than 200 photographs taken by the four cameras failed to reveal any corpses buried on the downs from the heat generated by the decomposing bodies or surrounding discoloured vegetation. The scientists were downcast that their 'super snooper' hadn't worked and the exercise hadn't been treated seriously. Wing Commander Wallis consoled himself with the fact his beloved autogyro appeared in the James Bond film *You Only Live Twice,* Q explaining to Bond how it worked so he could use rockets to destroy the baddies who conveniently turned up to attack him in fighter planes.

Sightings of Lucan flooded in from all over the world, hundreds of them. Some of them were taken seriously, others were obviously jokes: postcards from sunny climes signed 'Lucky' or 'L.L.' Casino registers all had their entries signed 'Lord Lucan'.

It wasn't only the authorities who were fooled into thinking the real Lucan had been spotted. It even happened to some of the newspapers. John Penrose went to the West Indies on behalf of the *Daily Mirror* and tailed a Lucan lookalike around an island for hours. He watched him eat a meal and carefully brought back a brandy glass with fingerprints on it that, unfortunately, did not match up. Owen Summers rushed off to South America after the *Daily Express* had a report Lucan was living in the mountains, tracking him down and bringing back a photograph which Veronica saw and had no hesitation in saying: 'That is not my husband. Also in the *Daily Express* the William Hickey column received a letter, supposedly from Harold Wilson's official residence at 10 Downing Street, typed on official headed notepaper but not signed. It said: *'Dear Hickey. Instead of being frivolous about the Lucan affair why not print the truth? It is an open secret that he escaped and is in Latin America. He did not mean to kill his children's nanny – he thought that she would be out that night – his motive was the custody of his children. Why have the public been deceived? With continuing support from cronies at the Clermont he will stay abroad and never return. Yours sincerely.'*

Right from the start Africa was the favourite venue as the bolthole of the lost Lucan. It would have been the easiest route to take, a journey across the English Channel, through France to Spain, a short sea crossing to Africa and down through countries where most of the authorities wouldn't have known or cared less about a murder in Britain. Lucan also had the cash sitting in the bank in Bulawayo, apparently a gift from the sort of generous aunt everyone would like to have. There was no reason why Lucan couldn't just turn up in Bulawayo and clean out the account, so from time to time we checked with Barclay's International that this hadn't happened and the money was still in the account.

Of the sightings on the Dark Continent there was one which I was prepared to keep an open mind about because an explanation was not forthcoming. It was made by a doctor in Cardiff Prison who told the authorities there he had met Lucan in Mozambique, the neighbouring country to what was then Rhodesia. They reported it to us and, on 6 June, I went to Cardiff to interview Dr Brian Hill. He was in jail facing charges of being involved in fraud over some land in Wales and, when I checked up with the police there, they said he was previously a

The Gorilla Man

perfectly respectable GP. He was totally sane and had nothing to gain. He did not want payment for the information, nor did he ask to do any sort of deal over his sentence as a reward for helping us.

What he said was that he went to South Africa on an engagement in Swaziland lasting several months and in April was making his way back to the UK via Mozambique. On the way his Land Rover was stopped, he reckoned, about seventeen times by Frelimo freedom fighters, but finally he arrived in the port of Lourenco Marques at midday, pleased to have got there in one piece. He booked into what was the best hotel in town, the Polono, and was sitting having a drink when a man and a woman came over to his table and started chatting about everything, including the political unrest in Mozambique. The man introduced himself as James and the girl as Maria. She spoke Portuguese and excellent but uncultured English. James was aged about thirty-nine to forty-five and Maria was in her early twenties. They said they were leaving Mozambique in a few days and were frightened because troops had arrested people in a neighbouring flat the night before. They had moved out of their flat and asked if they could stay in the doctor's room at the Polono. Dr Hill agreed, booking Maria in as his wife.

James said he knew Lourenco Marques well and would take him out to show him around. That night they went out to sleazy bars and nightclubs where James drank whisky and got increasingly more depressed. In the early hours of the morning James burst out crying, saying he couldn't go back to England and he was envious of the doctor because in a few days he would be leaving for home. When Dr Hill asked him why not, James replied: 'I can't go back, my name is Lord Lucan.' The doctor was mystified, saying: 'So what? Why can't you go back?' James explained that he was wanted in England and that he had escaped from the country by travelling from Newhaven to Dieppe on the ferry and from there had gone to Lisbon and on to Lourenco Marques. It all meant nothing to the doctor as he had been out of the country for some time and did not know anything about the murder and the hunt for Lucan.

In the morning Maria asked if he could run her to the airport, which he did, returning and meeting up again with James. It was a Saturday and James was jittery, saying a phone call would be made to the hotel in Dr Hill's name. This happened, and when the call came through the man on the end of the line sounded like an African. He passed the call to James and after about twenty minutes on the telephone he came back a far happier man. That evening they went out on the town again, this time James saying they had to be back early as he was being picked up about midnight. They got back to the hotel and Dr Hill went out for a walk. When he returned at 11.45 p.m. James was in the foyer with a black girl called Mary, who said she had met him when she was in England attending the London School of Economics. At that point a Mercedes drew up outside. Maria was in it with a black driver. James and Mary got in the car and they all disappeared into the night. Dr Hill never saw them again but, before he left, James had said he was heading through Tanganyika to Kenya and Mary would help him get through the border crossings. James had advised him to move to a different hotel and he had done this.

Dr Hill duly returned to England and it was only when he was in prison and saw a photograph of Lucan in the *Daily Express* that he recognized the man he knew as James in Lourenco Marques. I showed him our photographs and he said the man certainly closely resembled Lucan, taller than he was with black hair that looked artificially grey at the sides. There was no reason not to believe what Dr Hill said was true and that he had met someone in Lourenco Marques who claimed he was Lucan. But was the mysterious James the genuine missing earl? There were one or two things that didn't add up. James drank whisky while Lucan favoured vodka, though he had drunk whisky when Susan Maxwell-Scott gave it to him at her house. James was a non-smoker, whereas Lucan was a heavy smoker, and sleazy nightclubs weren't his usual haunts. It was also difficult to understand why, if James was Lucan, he would confide his travel plans to a man he had known only briefly who was returning to England and likely to tell the authorities he was making for Kenya. Surely Lucan wasn't that stupid. Was it just someone impersonating Lucan in order to get accommodation at the hotel? There was no way of knowing what it was all about.

As a result of what the doctor told us various messages were sent out to Mozambique and the surrounding countries through Interpol, together with a synopsis of the story. No replies were received, but this was not entirely surprising. There was usually little action taken by the African authorities on requests for assistance by other police forces.

17 The Inquest Verdict

The Sunday Times magazine appeared with the newspaper on 6 June, the result of weeks of painstaking inquiry by James Fox. I was among those who gave him background information because, with the hot pursuit having cooled off, I was anxious to give it fresh impetus. But it was Fox's own contacts as an Old Etonian within the Lucan circle that enabled him to put together the article that penetrated the wall of silence erected to protect Lucan. Fox was able to enlist the help of Dominic Elwes, who wanted no more than to present Lucan in a favourable light. John Aspinall cooperated for the same reason, saying Lucan was his fifth, sixth or seventh best friend and describing him as a warrior, a Roman who was quite capable of falling on his sword. It was a favoured phrase. I was told he used it at the lunch when the disappearance of Lucan was discussed. Falling on swords, shooting himself with a revolver, going down with the ship, why not a Japanese ritual disembowelling for good measure? It was always an honourable suicide. Nobody ever seemed to suggest Lucan would fling himself off a railway bridge under the wheels of the 7.10 to Crewe.

What Fox set out to do was not to glorify Lucan but to delve into whether he was, in truth, a bad hat who drove Veronica to the verge of a nervous breakdown. Fox spoke to the people who knew the couple and heard the rumours against Veronica that were in circulation and being regarded as the gospel truth. He spoke to Veronica and she told him of her isolation after the murder, weeks pacing the house going over and over the breakdown of her marriage and the awesome events of the night of 7 November. She described how she fought against voices she heard in her head telling her to kill herself because she was hallucinating from pills taken to stave off insomnia. It was powerful stuff, an excellent piece of investigative journalism, probing deep into Lucan's background and revealing how his parents had considered psychotherapy for him as a child because of an emotional disorder that gave him persistent headaches. Fox took readers behind the closed doors of the 'boys' clubs' where dwelt an unpleasant fraternity who resisted the intrusions of a prying public as they indulged in an alien lifestyle built on wealth and privilege and treated their womenfolk badly. The carefully contrived veneer of Lucan as a model husband was stripped away. It was Veronica who came across as a wronged woman more deserving of sympathy.

If the article upset Lucan's champions, the pictures that accompanied it were to cause an even greater furore. They were reproduced from the photo album that had been returned to Veronica from Lucan's flat, so I imagined she must have handed them to Fox. There was a two-page spread of the happy family snapshots of Lucan and Veronica with Gustav and Paula von Fürstenberg in Osnabrück, dining with friends at the El Morocco club in New York, and other photos taken at home of Lucan playing the piano and Veronica sitting on the bed. There was even one of the Doberman named Otto they had once owned, chewing on a bone. It was the other pictures that were to cause the trouble, the ones taken of Lucan after they split up and he went to Jimmy Goldsmith's birthday bash in Acapulco.

On the cover was the photo of Lady Annabel Birley in sunglasses and a straw hat with Lucan wearing a coral necklace over his shirt, her arm around his neck as she looked into his face. It was this picture, I was to learn later, that was to enrage Goldsmith when he saw the magazine in Sardinia, wrongly suggesting intimacy between Lady Annabel and Lucan. He was angry, too, at a painting which the impecunious Dominic Elwes had agreed to sell them for £200 to accompany the article appearing under the heading: THE LUCK OF THE LUCANS. It purported to show the Clermont scene and was a reconstruction of a group of diners at a table in the ornately-draped William Kent dining room. The painting may have been done especially for the article, or it might have been one he had done previously to amuse himself. Sitting at the long table were Lucan, Stephen Raphael, Charles Benson, the Earl of Suffolk, John Aspinall, Jimmy Goldsmith and Peter West, who worked for Goldsmith, while Nicholas Soames, grandson of Sir Winston Churchill, was standing. It was a crude sort of picture – Goldsmith with his arm raised as if summoning a waiter and only the back of Soames visible and looking for all the world like he was having a pee. The bizarre painting was bad enough as it illustrated an article critical of the Clermont set. What made it worse was that it could loosely be interpreted as being an artistic impression connected to the lunch called by John Aspinall on the day after the murder. The text mentioned the lunch, erroneously saying Jimmy Goldsmith was among those present. It was an unfortunate error in an otherwise largely accurate and fascinating summation of the Lucan saga that was to become the standard reference work on the subject.

It didn't take Goldsmith long to discover Elwes had painted the primitive picture and that he had played a part in assisting Fox to get material for the article. Elwes was also wrongly blamed for the photos getting into the hands of *The Sunday Times*. Goldsmith must have known who took the photographs in Acapulco. He himself was in some of them and must have seen who was behind the camera. It probably never occurred to anyone that Lucan had a set of prints and had tucked them in an album that would be given with his effects to Veronica. Perhaps it was even Elwes who took the snapshots, or it may have been his camera that was used to take them. That would account for the assumption that he sold them, along with the fact he was known to be short of money. But he didn't sell them to the newspaper. He would doubtless have recognized the pictures of Lady Annabel gazing adoringly at Lucan would be an act of betrayal that would infuriate Goldsmith and not go unpunished. Veronica, too, would be well aware the pictures showing Lady Annabel apparently linked romantically to Lucan would outrage Goldsmith, perhaps making him jealous and causing trouble between him and his mistress. That was probably Veronica's intention. She didn't like Lucan's friends and the pictures of her husband gambolling in Acapulco would further discredit him and point to his being responsible for the break-up of their marriage. This was a no-holds-barred game being played out, and an opportunity like that wouldn't go begging.

It was Elwes who was immediately cast in the role of Judas, despite Fox denying strenuously on his behalf that he was the source of the photographs but not naming the person who did provide them. He was actually more like Lazarus, who picked up crumbs from a rich man's table. Elwes was devastated when he was ostracised as a traitor by Goldsmith and his friends, Mark Birley writing him a letter saying he was being banned forthwith from his clubs, Annabel's and Mark's Club in Charles Street. Elwes apologized profusely to all and sundry for the part he did play, which Fox said was no more than anyone else and perhaps less than Aspinall. Elwes pleaded frantically to be forgiven and readmitted to the Goldsmith circle, all to no avail. There was no way back. Elwes was a brokenhearted reject, condemned as a social pariah for an act he didn't commit, an outcast from the people he cared most about and enjoyed making laugh.

The full inquest into the death of Sandra Rivett finally got under way on Monday, 16 June, having been put off once again from March by the Coroner, Dr Gavin Thurston. At the age of sixty-two he wasn't far off retirement and didn't relish a case that would be a legal minefield because of the feuding family and could easily add an unwanted stain to a distinguished career that included being deputy coroner to the Royal household. He said the extra time would enable inquiries to be continued and he hoped something more concrete would turn up. It didn't. His hopes that by June we would have Lucan lined up for an appearance in a criminal court proved to be wishful thinking. The inquest itself was going to be a murder trial after all. The basic tenet of British justice that a person was innocent of a crime until found guilty was in grave danger of being stood on its head, a danger presented by a coroner's court that had been recognized for decades. Coroners needed qualifications as both doctor and solicitor and Dr Thurston had written books on the subject, but a powerful arsenal of legal brains was being assembled for the inquest.

The James Fox article rekindled the smouldering embers of public interest in the Lucan case in the gossip columns. It also, as he wrote in a later article, resulted in a marked shift of feeling by reporters towards Veronica as a lonely, hard-done-by martyr and mother as the inquest was about to begin. So many journalists wanted to attend that their numbers had to be restricted because the courtroom in Horseferry Road was too small. They were not going to be disappointed. We had lined up a long list of more than thirty witnesses and the evidence was going to make compelling reading and build up to a cliff-hanging climax and the answer to the big question: Would

Lucan be named as a murderer by the jury? The stage was set. A crowd of onlookers would be waiting outside the court just as they were for the inquest on Brian Epstein, manager of The Beatles.

One witness who would not be giving evidence was Greville Howard, who produced a medical certificate to say he was in hospital and medically unfit to attend. He was the man who had made a statement to us disclosing a conversation with Lucan in which he said some time in advance of Sandra Rivett's murder that he planned to kill Veronica. It was the only signed affidavit we had of such a conversation and I was anxious to get him into the witness box so he could reveal it and nail Lucan as a murderer who premeditated the dastardly deed. Howard's disclosure had not improved his popularity rating among Lucan's partisans and I thought I would go the hospital for a medical report and to see if a speedy recovery was expected. Howard was ensconced in a private room at the Fitzroy Nuffield Hospital, a BUPA hospital in Marylebone, and I spoke to one of the sisters who was looking after him. She told me Howard was suffering from a mysterious back ailment she had never come across before, an agonizing and crippling condition which was baffling doctors and defying all attempts at a medical diagnosis. I reported my visit to Dr Thurston and asked him if there was anything he wanted me to do about it, like stretchering the stricken Howard into court or arranging a visit by the jury to his bed of pain. Dr Thurston said not to bother, he had enough evidence lined up from other witnesses to complete his inquiry without recourse to what Howard might have to say.

It was an unfortunate error of timing that the inquest was arranged to take place during Royal Ascot, highlight of the summer horse racing calendar when fashionable women parade in their finery. Being in the news for a week alongside Ascot was an irony the gambling Lucan would likely have appreciated before he lost his sense of humour. By their very nature inquests are normally sombre occasions where distraught relatives and friends show respect for their departed loved ones by dressing appropriately, sobbing women in black coats, men in similarly coloured ties. Sandra Rivett's inquest was different. Some of Lucan's adherents dressed up to the nines as if they were at the Queen's garden party or a summer fete on the village green. If their designer outfits and hats atop well-coiffured hair looked better suited to Ascot it wasn't surprising. That was where they were going when their presence wasn't required or the evidence promised to be technical and boring. Bill Shand Kydd said he had important business to attend to and was spied by the press tophatted in the Royal Enclosure to Ascot, his wife in a picture hat with a blue ostrich feather in it.

When questioned about playing hookey from the inquest to go to the races he explained it was at Ascot where he was doing his business. He was photographed one day as he left the courthouse beside Lucan's mother, the Dowager Countess, wearing a brightly patterned dress, both smiling as broadly as if they were emerging from a theatre. I took their demeanour to be deliberate, their unconcern a public display telling the world Lucan had nothing to do with Sandra's death so why should they be perturbed at her inquest. It was either that or a flagrant example of the upper classes not caring a jot for the fate of a mere servant.

During lunch recesses throughout the inquest the Lucan clan would go across the road to the Barley Mow public house right opposite the courtroom and eat well at reserved tables in the upstairs restaurant while we mingled with the reporters below in the bar. In court the family studiously ignored the small figure of Veronica sitting in a row behind them in her black velvet coat, creating an atmosphere of stark animosity you could cut with a knife. James Fox wrote that the courtroom bristled with the hostilities of Veronica's relatives towards her and he was right. Even her own sister, Christina Shand Kydd, gave her the cold shoulder, as did her sister-in-law Sally Gibbs. Veronica was all alone, an outsider banished from the family she had been proud to belong to but had never really been accepted into with open arms. While they all trooped over to the pub with their legal representatives, Veronica would go off with Sgt Forsyth somewhere else, possibly to the sanctuary of the Duke of Boots. Like the bright clothes and contrived bonhomie, the Lucan family seemed to have a calculated policy in coldly shunning Veronica, a subtle message demonstrating she was to blame for the failure of her marriage and the evidence she would give at the inquest was not to be believed.

As for the members of Sandra Rivett's family, her father, Albert Hensby, aunt, Mrs Vera Ward, and sister Charmaine sat quietly and almost unnoticed in a corner at the back of the

The Inquest Verdict

packed and stiflingly-hot courtroom. Her mother stayed at home because she was unable to face the harrowing ordeal of hearing the gory details of how Sandra was beaten to death. Mr Hensby got increasingly angry as it soon became clear the inquest on his daughter was in reality going to be a trial, Sandra's death relegated to a sideshow in a battle to stop Lucan being labelled a murderer. If that happened it would be the first time since 1765 when the 'wicked' Lord Byron, great uncle of the poet, was convicted for killing a cousin in a quarrel at a club dinner, but exempted from punishment as a peer.

Hensby, a factory worker, was dismayed, complaining bitterly to the press: 'My daughter's name has hardly been mentioned, yet she is the reason we are all here. She was a kind, gentle person who loved children and wouldn't hurt anyone.' Mrs Ward, who helped us considerably in our inquiries over the death of her niece, hit the nail on the head when she said: 'I am appalled. Sandra is supposed to be the central figure, but her name has hardly come up. It is like the shopgirl and the prince. They make Sandra seem that she didn't matter. Sandra is in the middle of what seems to be a battle between the two sides of the Lucan family. Meawhile, it is Sandra who died and she is gone and forgotten.'

As at Balaclava, an impressive force of combatants squared up against one another for the fight that would be fought to a conclusion over four days. Michael Eastham, a top Queen's Counsel, represented the Lucan family, his battle orders to advance over the difficult legal terrain and show Veronica was lying in her teeth. Veronica's defensive barriers were manned by Bruce Coles, another skilled QC, tasked with making sure her barricades were not breached. Sandra Rivett's family were also represented by counsel, David Webster, and the Commissioner of Police of the Metropolis by Brian Watling, both basically supporting the defenders. Other legal eagles watched from the hills above the battlefield, protecting their flanks as the Heavy Brigades slugged it out in the valley below.

It was for the Coroner to decide on the rules of engagement. Mr Thurston carefully explained to the jury of six men and three women exactly what it was they were charged to do and the legal constraints on evidence that a wife could give against her husband. I knew from my discussions with Mr Thurston he had pondered long and hard on whether he should even put

Veronica on the witness stand, deciding in the end he would, but determined to try and stop the quarrelling family engaging in a disorderly melée. 'This is not a trial,' he stressed optimistically.

Mr Thurston was right to be uneasy. Mr Eastham fired off a range finding shot as soon as he got to his feet to question Veronica after she had given her evidence naming Lucan as her attacker. 'The separation was in January 1973, but even before that you entertained feelings of hatred for your husband, did you not?' he asked bluntly.

It brought the response he was doubtless expecting, Mr Coles leaping straight to his feet to protest: 'I don't know how this can help the inquiry.' The Coroner agreed, saying it was a strong way of putting it. There followed a discussion on the contents of the letter Lucan wrote to Bill Shand Kydd, Mr Eastham pointing out that it said Veronica had demonstrated her 'hatred' to him in the past. The Coroner countered by saying Lucan had also mentioned 'ghastly circumstances' so it sounded like he was under stress when he wrote the letter.

Mr Eastham decided to launch a full frontal attack, saying he wanted to establish the relationship between Lucan and his wife. This involved the inescapable and unpleasant duty of suggesting that what she was saying she knew to be untrue. He said he had a heavy responsibility on his shoulders because the only case he could put forward was based on what Lucan said to his mother and Mrs Maxwell Scott and wrote in the letters. While he would undertake to limit his questions as far as he could, it was essential he obtained sufficient evidence for the jury to properly realize the issue they would have to consider.

With his big guns fired Mr Eastham had to sit back and wait to see what effect they would have as the Coroner sent out the jury while the lawyers engaged in a hand-to-hand legal skirmish. The argument went against him. Mr Thurston decided the relationship of Lucan and Veronica was outside the terms of the inquest. When the jury were called back in after fifteen minutes Mr Eastham said disconsolately: 'In view of the ruling you have given in the absence of the jury, I do not think I can assist the jury at all, and I do not wish to ask the lady any questions.'

Family tensions were again exposed when Kait, the Dowager Countess, gave her evidence, affirming as an agnostic instead of taking the oath. She spoke of a conversation with Christina Shand Kydd in which she told her Veronica was in hospital and she commented: 'Has she attempted to kill herself again?' This recollection brought Mr Coles jumping to his feet to protest. The Coroner said he would not record the comment as it was prejudicial and he requested the press not to report it.

The ruling that nothing would be admissible that would be seen to discredit Veronica devastated Mr Eastham's battle plan. It also resulted in some unusual and ridiculous questioning because witnesses would be confined to only yes and no answers if anything on these lines was raised. When Bill Shand Kydd was questioned by Mr Eastham about the letter he received from Lucan he was prevented from giving an explanation of what it meant. Yes, he said, he could say more about how Veronica had demonstrated her hatred towards Lucan. Yes, the line about explaining to the children the dream of paranoia did make sense to him when he read it and he knew what Lucan was getting at.

I was none the wiser and neither were the jury, who were becoming increasingly aware the ground rules were preventing them from hearing all the facts. Witnesses were being gagged and they were being asked to decide whether or not Lucan murdered Sandra. Apart from the rules imposed by the Coroner they were faced with the law which said Veronica could only give evidence against Lucan in relation to his attack on her. Veronica had not been able to tell them anything about what she knew about the body of Sandra being in the basement. Clearly frustrated the foreman, William Thomas, said: 'We have heard nothing at all from Lady Lucan about the nanny being murdered. We heard about her going to the Plumbers Arms and saying "*He has murdered my nanny*". But how did she know the nanny had been murdered?' Dr Thurston could only dodge the question, saying: 'That is right. I suggest we hear the rest of the evidence, then I hope to be able to satisfy you on that.' At least the rival forces were each fighting with an arm tied behind their back but, whoever won, the loser would have cause for complaint and the law made to look an ass.

One after another we all went into the witness box to give our evidence and face questions. I described the experiments we had carried out to show what could be seen through the window of 46 Lower Belgrave Street. When most of the witnesses had been called there was still no sign Greville Howard was going to be declared fit enough to take the stand. We made a final attempt to get his statement admitted as evidence by having it read out in his absence. The jury were again asked to leave the courtroom while Mr Watling made his submission. He said Mr Eastham had made great play during the hearing of a 'third person' being involved and the statement by Howard would provide evidence of Lucan's depressed state of mind, something that was highly relevant and should be before the jury. As I expected, Mr Eastham said he strongly objected because there would be no opportunity to cross-examine Howard in court and the Coroner upheld his argument.

There was another backstage legal debate after the final witness was called and the jury were dismissed for the day. The Coroner was still concerned about the question the jury had asked about how Veronica knew Sandra had been murdered. Mr Thurston said he proposed to recall Veronica to the witness box and ask her what was said after her fight with Lucan. Mr Eastham was aghast and again protested strongly, referring to the law on wife's evidence and saying, coming at the end of the hearing, it would have a devastating prejudicial effect and would bar Lucan forever from getting a fair trial. Even Mr Coles had to concede this point and Mr Thurston decided to drop the idea. The jury would not be told from Veronica's own mouth. They would not get their answer; instead they would have to draw their conclusions from the rest of the evidence they had heard on why she burst into the Plumbers Arms and said Sandra had been murdered. In his summing up Mr Thurston told them: 'I'm going to ask you to dismiss it from your minds. You should not speculate as to how it came about this was said. You should not draw any inference in any direction from this remark. The only person who can clarify this point is Lady Lucan and she is, in this context, debarred from clearing the matter up with you.'

Before reviewing the evidence Dr Thurston told the jury: 'It is fairly clear from the letters written by Lord Lucan that there is existing in the family animosity, tension and matters which, if aired, could only be prejudicial and painful to those concerned. To raise family tensions would not benefit this inquiry. If these matters could further the inquiry into Sandra Rivett's death then I would take a different view. Simply to turn this into a forum for airing family tensions would be wrong. I do not think justice would be served by doing so.'

Concluding a summary that lasted over an hour, Dr Thurston

said to the jury: 'I do not think in this case I can ask you to consider the question of accidental death, or any other finding that these injuries were inflicted by some unknown person. The circumstances are quite clear. If you are satisfied on the evidence there was an attack by another person, your verdict would have to be murder. I cannot see how on this evidence I can possibly offer you any alternative. You have to ascertain the person, or persons, if any, to be charged with murder or manslaughter. On the evidence, you have got to decide whether you feel you can name the person responsible.'

It took just over half-an-hour for the jury to reach their verdict. They filed back in and foreman William Thomas rose to his feet and announced: 'Murder by Lord Lucan.' The jury had done it, named Richard John Bingham, Earl of Lucan, as a murderer. Dr Thurston told them: 'It is a rare procedure in coroners' courts for a person to be named as you have done. It is my duty to commit that person for trial to the Central Criminal Court. In this case there is nobody I can commit because we don't known where Lord Lucan is. There is no doubt if he turns up he will be charged.'

18 Chasing False Trails

The inquest verdict naming Lucan as a murderer was expected. It was the only verdict the jury could bring in apart from murder by a person or persons unknown. It was totally unjust in that no full defence was given on his behalf, a fact finally recognized with a change in the law later so that inquest juries could no longer name a murderer. I sat through the whole inquest in the small old-fashioned courtroom, astonished at how Veronica kept her composure, her face expressionless as she sat listening impassively as the drama unfolded. When it was over, I thanked Dr Thurston for his courtesy and cooperation throughout the many preparation meetings we had together, some at his London home, assembling the witnesses and exhibits he would require. Then I went for a drink with the coroner's officers at the Barley Mow. Dr Thurston was a kindly man; his staff thought the world of him. The shock waves from the sensational result quickly spread out and Dr Thurston came in for some criticism. I thought Dr Thurston handled the inquest well, given his limited legal experience and the calibre of the big guns he was facing. He tried to achieve a result without too much prejudicing any future criminal proceedings – an impossible task. Because the inquest itself became a quasi trial, the Lucan family were unhappy at not being able to mount a stout defence, challenging evidence, producing witnesses and advancing arguments to prove his innocence. Nothing at the inquest would have satisfied them short of Veronica on the witness stand being savaged under cross-examination over her mental state, her hatred of Lucan and the untrustworthiness of her memory of the night because of confusion by being hit about the head. Lucan's brother-in-law, the Revd William Gibbs, told reporters: 'If the jury has the power to decide who is guilty of a murder, then by what right does the Coroner refuse to hear evidence to the

Chasing False Trails

contrary? The coroner several times prevented questions that would have helped Lord Lucan. To me it is amazing and frightening a coroner's court jury can name a man a murderer without hearing all the relevant evidence. This is not British justice and therefore must be ignored.'

Reactions to the verdict were equally predictable from the other parties involved. Veronica issued a brief statement through a solicitor which said: 'I am obviously very relieved that the coroner's inquiry is over. I intend to put the past behind me so far as I can and continue to lead a family life. As to the inquiry, you have heard the evidence. My husband's interests were represented before the coroner and the jury have returned their verdict. I cannot say that I am pleased or displeased with the verdict. I was concerned only with establishing the facts.'

At least the Hensby family whose daughter was the real victim of the drama were satisfied with the verdict. Mrs Hensby said: 'Thank God they have returned the right verdict. I was so afraid they would say my darling daughter was murdered by someone unknown. For days I have prayed this would come about. I wanted Lord Lucan named as the man who killed my daughter. I would like to think he is dead, but I believe he is still alive somewhere. He has so many friends with so much money.'

The press was delighted, taking the verdict as if Lucan had been found guilty in a criminal court to write what they liked about him. I was pleased the inquest was finally over because it had involved a lot of work. The result was satisfactory in that the evidence we had gathered had convinced a jury Lucan was guilty, but it had not been tested under fierce cross-examination and they had not heard Lucan's version of events. The inquest appeared to be a conclusion in that a verdict against Lucan was reached and the public had the answers to many questions previously unpublished. It ignored the central fact that Lucan was still at liberty and our hunt for him would go on.

The day after the inquest finished Roy Ranson and I were summoned to Scotland Yard to see the Deputy Assistant Commissioner. He told us that while the inquest was on Interpol had received word that a man exactly answering Lucan's description had been seen in Cherbourg, the port on the French side of the cross-channel ferry service from Southampton. According to the message Lucan had stayed for a few days at a hotel near the ferry terminal. The description was so accurate it was decided we should go across to France and investigate.

Detective Chief Superintendent Stan Pittaway, the officer in charge of Interpol at Scotland Yard, introduced us to a woman who worked for him, Glynne Rhys-Evans, an attractive 40-year-old ex-Indian Airline stewardess who had travelled all over the world and spoke fluent French. It was agreed she would accompany us as our interpreter. At Southampton we met Special Branch officers who introduced us to the ship's purser on the *Viking 1*. We questioned him about the type of people who used the ship and interviewed some of the officers and crew to see if any of them had any recollections of seeing anyone like Lucan on board. As we sailed across the channel in glorious June sunshine we were unaware we were embarking on a press party that would become a legend in Fleet Street.

Unlike in films, policemen are not able to travel from country to country, wandering about asking questions of who they like. In France there is an official pattern to be followed and we had to go before the instructing judge of the local court to get what they called a 'commission rogatoire' by producing a letter from the Director of Public Prosecutions office. This satisfied the French love for bureaucratic red tape and entitled us to interview people, provided we were accompanied by a local officer who would take down any written statements we needed to have. Armed with the piece of paper we set about interviewing various people. After two days, the local CID office said the British Consul wanted to see us, and he wasn't a happy man. We went to the consulate office and were ushered into his office to see him. Reggie Rogers, Her Majesty's representative in Cherbourg, reminded me of Sydney Greenstreet in *The Maltese Falcon*, overweight and continually mopping his sweating forehead in the hot weather. He chided us for not letting him know we were in Cherbourg and, after apologies all round for our discourtesy, he produced a bottle of Scotch and gave us a few tots, offering us any help he could give. As not much had happened in his little domain for a long time he didn't want to miss out on the action.

By then the press corps had hit town in large numbers. TV and radio crews and the cream of Fleet Street's crime and feature writers were on the rampage after word had got out where we had gone. We held a press conference in the canteen of the police station and told them what we planned to do. They were in high spirits, determined on a monumental binge and celebrating the inquest verdict that they saw as removing the shackles on what they could say about Lucan. It was open season on Lucan – he was fair game for whatever they cared to write and the hunt had suddenly turned into farce. Lord Luck, the *Daily Express* astrologer, wrote: 'While on the run Lord Lucan will have a natural instinct for survival – the instinct of a hunted animal. Born a Sagittarius, he is the kind of person who will keep running and never give himself up voluntarily. He will be extremely self-reliant and under normal conditions would keep himself well under control. Rather than give himself up he will have to be cornered. This is the Sagittarius instinct. Under the conditions he is now facing he will have a tremendous capacity for action. He will run until he drops.'

The focus of attention in Cherbourg was Mme Suzanne Guilpain, red-headed proprietress of Le Grand Hotel, a two-star hotel near the ferry terminal that belied its name. She sparked off our visit by claiming Lucan had stayed at her hotel three times, the last time skipping off without paying. We interviewed her, showed her a copy of *The Sunday Times* magazine, and she said the photographs did look like her English guest. From her description it didn't sound much like Lucan. She said the man smelt dirty and spoke perfect French with a Parisian accent. This ruled out Lucan because he could only speak passable schoolboy French and I couldn't imagine him being dirty, even on the run. But her report was good for her business in the middle of the holiday season. It was John Knight from the *Sunday Mirror* who managed to book into Room 22, the one Lucan was supposed to have used. He wrote: 'We seek him here, we seek him there, we seek the loathsome Lucan everywhere.' Knight peered under the bed without finding Lucan and searched through the drawers of the little bedside writing table. He reported there were no half-written letters from Lucan to his friends saying he was having to 'lie doggo'. Looking from his window Knight did not think the little boats in the harbour were grand enough to be used by Lucan's friends coming from England to give him funds.

Not to be outdone in earning some free publicity and a few francs, another photographic French woman, Mme Brigitte

Caremoli, claimed Lucan had dined on oysters and steak with a dark-haired twenty-something girl at her mother's restaurant, the Ancre d'Or, not far from the Grand Hotel. She said the pair left without leaving a tip, a detail I took to be a sly dig at the Brits. By all accounts we didn't have a good reputation for generosity and paying our hotel bills.

In order to give as much coverage as possible to our visit we were invited by a French TV station to appear on an early evening magazine programme broadcast from Caen. We flew there from the airport at Cherbourg in a little plane that could only carry six people. It took off and headed up into the blue sky, giving us an impressive view of the Normandy coastline where the Allied armies landed on D-Day. I thought it was odd when the plane turned and we started heading straight out to sea, the pilot babbling away excitedly into the microphone of his radio. He suddenly turned round grim faced and said something to Glynne, which she translated. 'He says we're lost, he can't find the airfield,' she said. 'Can we please look out of the window? He says we're bound to spot it because there is a Cross of Lorraine marked on the ground.' We turned round and flew back towards the coast and, sure enough, someone finally spotted the cross mowed into the grass of Caen airfield, which was otherwise about six feet deep on the runway controlled by a tin nissen hut acting as a control tower. At the TV studios Roy Ranson was interviewed and told viewers why we were in France, sparking off a fresh rash of Lucan sightings up and down the coast.

By the time we went to check a sighting by a Scots woman at the Hotel Central in St Malo, the French police were getting thoroughly sick of Lucan. As we had moved into a different police area in Brittany we again had to go back to the local Palace of Justice to get written authority. The police in St Malo weren't used to being hassled by a marauding pack of foreign pressmen taking the mickey. The officer who drove us around St Malo didn't like being followed everywhere and came in for particular ribbing. He had the misfortune to have long arms and a short body and the briefcase and typewriter he carried dragged along the ground. When he parked his tiny Renault car some distance from the hotel and forgot exactly where, it was an opportunity too good to be missed. Helpful reporters directed him all over the town. The Central Hotel proved to be another

Chasing False Trails

dead end – we checked the register and interviewed eight members of staff, but none of them remembered seeing Lucan. While we were in the area we took the opportunity to visit the casino in nearby Dinard but none of the staff there had seen Lucan. I wasn't surprised. The casino was very modest, not a patch on the Clermont. If Lucan was abroad and reduced to gambling in casinos like this one, I thought, he would do well to return home, give himself up and do his porridge.

On Saturday night, at the end of a hectic week, we and a group from the press who had stayed the course hosted a slap-up dinner in one of the seafront bars in Cherbourg to say 'thank you' to the local police. The British Consul was guest of honour and thoroughly enjoyed himself. We didn't find any trace of Lucan but Les Anglais showed the French they are not the only ones who know how to have a good time. James Fox wrote that the intake of alcohol made the trip look more like a wine tasting expedition which had gone madly out of control than a serious search for Lucan, adding it was a mystery to those newsmen present how a single line of copy was filed. That was a gross canard and distortion of the facts by the usually reliable scribe, doubtless brought about by an attack of sour grapes at not being on the earnest excursion into darkest France. Owen Summers quoted me in the *Daily Express* as saying: 'We have established good relations with French police helping us in the world-wide search for Lucan – so the exercise cannot be regarded as a failure.' I was proud of that, I thought it was rather well put.

On Sunday the *QE2*, the world's most famous super liner, docked in Cherbourg and the Special Branch officers who travel on it from Southampton gave us a guided tour of the ship. They showed us the ship's newspaper produced for passengers to read crossing the Atlantic which contained an article on our search for Lucan at Cherbourg. The *QE2* – had we thought of that as Lucan's means of escape? That would surely be more his style, not a ferry boat. I ran my eye carefully over the passengers strolling on the deck in the sunshine.

While we were on the northern coast of France, Dominic Elwes was down in the south at St Jean Cap Ferrat, not far from Monte Carlo. He was staying as a house guest at the Villa Palladium, a villa owned by the Marquis of Northampton. Among those who attended a party hosted by Lord Compton, son and heir to the Marquis, was John Deen, whose family owned the Blue Circle garages. Old Etonian Deen owned racehorses and the previous week had been at Royal Ascot. His brother Rupert was one of the people on the fringes of the aristocracy in Belgravia. Once or twice a month he would drop in to see me and we would have a drink in my office or go round to the Duke of Boots. I got to know Rupert because of his association with Lady Charlotte Curzon, daughter of Lord Howe, who was regularly in the gossip columns. Earl Howe, a charming man who had been a racing driver in the 1930s, used to say to me: 'Please, what can you do about Charlotte.' I'd say to him: 'I'm sorry, my Lord, she's your daughter, there's not a lot I can do. She's not a juvenile, she's over eighteen, provided she doesn't break the law I can't tell her what to do.'

On one occasion Charlotte had a row with her boyfriend, a London car dealer named George Wright who the police kept an eye on. He loosed off her shotgun out the window of her mews cottage and peppered the garage doors of the Belgian Embassy, causing a minor diplomatic incident. The Ambassador did not take it further, but Charlotte had her shotgun licence taken away. There was another incident involving Wright when he went into Annabel's where Charlotte was dining with friends and he ended up in hospital for treatment to cuts. Wright, like Elwes, was to die in 1977 from a drugs overdose at the age of thirty-eight. Earl Howe's daughter Sarah, known as Sally, was widowed at the age of twenty-three when her racing driver husband, Piers Courage, was killed in a crash. In 1972 she became the third wife of John Aspinall.

I learned from James Fox that Elwes was sent to the Villa Palladium by Daniel Meinertzhagen because he thought he was cracking up from the strain of being barred from his favourite London haunts. Elwes flew down to the Mediterranean on Friday, 16 June, the day the newspapers were filled with the inquest verdict on Lucan. At Heathrow airport as he was catching a flight to Nice he bumped into *Daily Mail* columnist Nigel Dempster and told him tearfully how Goldsmith was blaming him for selling the photographs to the *Sunday Times*. Dempster took pity on him and tried to ring Goldsmith to tell him Elwes was being wrongly accused. He could not speak to Goldsmith directly so had a secretary pass on a message.

It was from the Villa Palladium that overwrought Elwes made an extraordinary plea in a story in the *Daily Express*, written by Don Coolican and Frank Thorne, for Lucan to come out of hiding and get in touch with him. He said he was one of Lucan's best friends. They were almost like brothers and had been in daily touch during their fifteen-year friendship. 'If Lucky did contact me I would tell him to go to the police and sort this whole bloody mess out,' he said. 'I am sure he is still alive somewhere and hiding in the most desperate circumstances. I and the rest of his friends would like to help him and do our duty as far as the law is concerned. Why, oh why, doesn't he get in touch with us?'

Later in the front page lead story Elwes said: 'I've been so worried about Lucky that I've almost reached a state of depression. He must telephone me. Why doesn't he get in touch with me? My other friends in London realise the sort of pressure I have been under. This is a ghastly business with police asking me questions all the time. My good friend Lord Compton offered me this refuge to disappear to. I still cannot relax, though, even though I am totally alone. I feel so lost.'

19   The Goldenballs Case

The visit to the Cote d'Azure did nothing to raise the spirits of Elwes despite cruising on the luxury yacht *Bulldog* owned by industrialist Jimmy Hanson. It may have been he knew there was no escape from the shadow of Lucan. The French police were scouring the Corniche looking for him among the villas dotting the hillside and the crowded yacht marinas. If his impassioned plea for Lucan to contact him reached the ears of the on-the-run earl he did not respond. Nor did Jimmy Goldsmith or Mark Birley give any indication he was likely to be readmitted to the fold. Either his denial over selling the photographs wasn't believed or his sin in cooperating at all over the article and selling the painting was a sufficient transgression in itself. There may have even been another reason I knew nothing about. To my mind Elwes may have been indiscreet, but he was being asked to pay a heavy price for what seemed an innocuous violation of a code of ethics his friends had adopted for themselves.

After a short stay at the Villa Palladium, Elwes went to Spain where he owned some land he was trying to develop in the Province of Cadiz at El Cuartom, Tarifa. There he slipped down a cliff and hurt himself. When he returned to England at the end of August, Elwes was a physical and emotional mess, his depressed mood not helped by his father being terminally ill and his mother in a psychiatric home being looked after by nuns. The barriers were still up, he was still *persona non grata* at Annabel's and Mark's Club, presumably at Goldsmith's behest because Birley had no great cause to be incensed. Birley hadn't featured in the *Sunday Times* spread at all and the cover photograph of his wife looking at Lucan was scarcely likely to bother him too much as she had long been the mistress of Goldsmith. Whatever the reason, Elwes was still blackballed, drummed out of the Brownies.

The Goldenballs Case

Like Lucan when faced with an emotional mid-life crisis, Elwes was hitting the bottle hard and having trouble sleeping. He asked a friend to pick up some Tuinal tablets he was having on prescription from a pharmacy in Knightsbridge and drop them through the letter box of the flat where he was living off the King's Road. Weighed down with depression he took all the barbiturate tablets, washing them down with alcohol. His close friend Melissa Wyndham, an interior decorator, let herself into his flat on 5 September when he failed to answer the telephone. She found Elwes lying dead on his bed from a massive overdose. Beside him were two suicide notes, one of which read: 'I curse Mark and Jimmy from the grave. I hope they are happy now.' At his inquest, ironically held by Dr Thurston in the same courtroom as that of Sandra Rivett where Lucan was branded a murderer, he decided against disclosing the contents of the letters, but what Elwes wrote as his life ebbed away became known to journalists. Dr Thurston felt there was no question his death was an accident and he recorded a verdict that Elwes killed himself. After hearing the evidence he said it sounded like Elwes had a manic-depressive personality and so suicide was always a risk.

A memorial service for Dominic Elwes was held in Mayfair at the Church of Our Lady of the Immaculate Conception in Farm Street on 25 November. It was well attended, a tribute to the regard he was held in by his real friends, not those whose popularity he sought and who finally rejected him. Among those at the service was Graham Hill, twice world champion racing driver, who, sadly, was himself to die just four days later. The small plane he was piloting crashed in bad weather at Elstree in Hertfordshire on a flight from Marseilles, killing Hill and members of his racing team. Hill had his own Piper Aztec plane and, as a racing driver, was not lacking in nerve, but there was no reason for us to think he was involved in flying Lucan out of the country. Lucan had many friends with planes and boats; any one of them could have helped him escape.

In one of his suicide notes Elwes had asked that his friend Kenneth Tynan, the well-known theatre critic and impresario, should speak at the service. He did, in a warm and widely reported eulogy with carefully chosen words that did nothing to disguise his dislike of the people whose company Elwes had coveted. Tynan said: 'His laughter, which still rings in my ears, was a triumphant yelp of victory, a cackle of conquest, over drabness and pretension. People of quite remarkable ordinariness are permanently lodged in my mind because of the skill with which they were sketched by this superb verbal cartoonist. As a raconteur and mimic, he had the most ebullient and imaginative flair I have ever encountered. Nobody has ever made me rejoice more. Even Peter Ustinov, a superlative talker, is reputed to have said Dominic was the only person to whom he would defer in conversation. He loved the world of wealth and ceremony far more than it deserved, and his politics were those of a romantic monarchist. For him, England's king over the water was the Duke of Windsor. Certain people elected him their court jester, and he happily embraced the role. But they never really accepted him because, in the final analysis, he did not have quite enough money. It may be he set too much store by the favourable opinions of people, many of whom were manifestly his inferiors.'

Tynan was followed to the pulpit by John Aspinall, who Elwes had also requested to give an oration. Elwes knew Aspinall to be a gifted speaker and, knowing also his disregard for convention and his views on genetics, would probably not have been surprised at the address he gave. Aspinall described Elwes's failure to make money as a genetic flaw. He said Elwes resented the fact many lesser men had found fame through the media and through newspapers. Elwes knew many people who had achieved much, but he himself never managed it, nor were his business affairs the success they might have been. Aspinall said Elwes had been happiest entertaining a dozen or more close friends with his amusing stories or his wit. Unfortunately, he said, modern society did not repay someone like Elwes. It was the man who could entertain television audiences with banalities who got rewarded.

Aspinall was typically unorthodox, mentioning the word 'genetics' at least four times in a passionate eulogy, unlike anything usually heard in the Jesuit church. He said Elwes had been from a long line of Saxons who yearned for posthumous fame and he would have it in the immortality of his genes. Elwes, he said, had been like a bard in an Anglo-Saxon court. He had described the events of the day to the assembled lords in entertaining fashion, 'unlocking the word hoard' as it had been put in the epic 6th Old English poem about the Scandinavian folk hero Beowulf. Aspinall quoted from Cicero and he quoted from Oscar Wilde, even adding a poem of his own which began: 'Why did you leave us Dominic? Why did you die?'

It was a powerful eulogy, intended to laud Elwes in a way Aspinall thought his friend would appreciate. He must have known that what he said and the forceful way in which he expressed it as a natural showman would stun some members of the congregation. Elwes's family apparently took the address in the spirit it was intended. They recognized that, in asking Aspinall to make it, Elwes was well aware it would be unconventional and he would have been delighted by it. Others who heard it thought Aspinall had been utterly insensitive and tasteless in his remarks, particularly in suggesting Elwes had not been equipped to deal with life because of his genetic inheritance and knowing the misery he went through and the tragic circumstances of his death. They knew, too, Aspinall was one of the rich people who Tynan had been alluding to in his address. As Aspinall left the church, Tremayne Rodd, a godson of Elwes's mother, punched him on the jaw, saying: 'That's what I think of your bloody speech, Aspinall.' Rubbing his jaw, Aspinall retorted: 'I am used to this sort of thing in dealing with wild animals.' The incident was witnessed by the press and photographs were taken of Aspinall holding his bruised jaw. In the *Daily Mail* the next day the heading on the story said: RIGHT HOOK ENDS MEMORIAL SERVICE TO MAN FROM LUCAN SET. There was to be no respite for Elwes from the shadow of Lucan, even beyond the grave.

It was the demise of Elwes, following on from James Fox's *Sunday Times* article, that aroused the curiosity of Richard Ingrams, editor of *Private Eye* magazine. Aspinall getting punched after his oration at the Elwes requiem mass whetted his interest that there was more to the aftermath of the Lucan case than met the eye. He was particularly intrigued because the affair featured Jimmy Goldsmith and came at the same time he was in the news for his business dealings, having taken over the chairmanship of the troubled Slater Walker financial empire. Jim Slater's early resignation on 24 October shocked the City, and the Bank of England stepped in with a financial lifeboat and Goldsmith at the helm. Ingrams was also interested in the fact that Greville Howard, missing witness at the Sandra Rivett inquest, worked for Goldsmith at Slater Walker. Howard had also been Goldsmith's personal assistant at Cavenham some time before, though Ingrams said he didn't know that at the time. Ingrams asked one of the magazine's writers, Patrick Marnham, to look into the background and write a story, concentrating on the part played by Goldsmith.

The full-page piece Marnham wrote appeared in December under the heading *All's Well That Ends Elwes* and was to lead to lengthy litigation and bring the magazine to the brink of closure. What *Private Eye* did not know was James Fox had been wrong in the first place in naming Goldsmith as being at the lunch at Aspinall's house after Lucan disappeared. They compounded the error by assuming Goldsmith would have taken control as the richest and most powerful person in the group and must therefore have played a part in any conspiracy. In the story Marnham wrote: 'From the beginning, the police have met obstruction and silence from the circle of gamblers and boneheads with whom Lord Lucan and Dominic Elwes associated.' The use of the word 'obstruction' was also unfortunate, suggesting as it did a criminal offence had been committed.

Goldsmith issued a total of sixty-three writs against the magazine and thirty-seven of its distributors, alleging libel. The distributors split about evenly, seventeen deciding to fight the action, but it cost the magazine an immediate loss of eight per cent of its circulation. Goldsmith also swore an affidavit alleging Criminal Libel, a rarely invoked procedure carrying a prison sentence. He complained the article suggested there was a conspiracy among Lucan's friends to obstruct the course of justice and to assist the fugitive earl, and that he had played a leading and dominant part. It also suggested Elwes was compelled against his will to visit Lady Lucan in hospital to discover what she had told the police and Howard had been pressured and persuaded to evade giving evidence at the inquest.

Court procedures dragged on for many months, *Private Eye* paying for their costs with a 'Goldenballs' fund to which all kinds of people contributed. Goldsmith eventually won the civil libel action and received his public apology. The Criminal Libel case ended with Ingrams and Marnham pronounced Not Guilty by agreement at the Old Bailey after an apology was published in an advertisement in the *Evening Standard*, part of which read: '*Private Eye* now recognises that any suggestion in the issue of 12th December 1975 that Sir James had taken part in a criminal conspiracy was particularly serious, and wishes to make it known publicly once and for all that there was not a shred of truth in it.' *Private Eye* also agreed to pay substantial costs, but Goldsmith was miffed when Ingrams did not fulfil a third condition, that they should have lunch together.

There was an amusing sidelight in the case when it was admitted at one of the hearings by Goldsmith's barrister, Lewis Hawser, QC, that a reputable firm of private investigators had rummaged in *Private Eye*'s dustbins for information, photocopying papers and putting them back to avoid allegations of theft. It tickled me as I was investigating the theft of Prime Minister Harold Wilson's papers amid his allegations of a 'dirty tricks' campaign being mounted against him. Ingrams claimed in his book about the legal battle, *Goldenballs*, that Harold Wilson offered newspapers a list of *Private Eye* informers and this could only have been compiled with the help of the dustbin scavengers.

20 Last Refuge of a Scoundrel

By the time the inquest on Sandra Rivett was over and Lucan was named a murderer, opinion was equally divided on whether or not he was still alive. Roy Ranson was certain he was dead, his body lost in the English Channel. I was equally convinced he was alive, his escape engineered by his friends. Officers of the murder squad were equally split down the middle on the issue. The majority of Lucan's friends said they thought he was dead, but Dominic Elwes was a notable exception because he had appealed to his friend to reveal himself.

I had many reasons for believing Lucan was alive, not least the fact his body wasn't found. Nor could I see he had reason to commit suicide, other than the shame of his children seeing him in the dock charged with murder. I don't think the murder of Sandra Rivett itself would have so traumatized him he would become suicidal. His ancestor, the 3rd Earl of Lucan, had a great deal more blood on his hands and it's doubtful the thought ever crossed *his* mind. If Lucan was prepared to live with the death of Veronica on his conscience he could certainly exist untroubled by the death of Sandra. Lucan was supremely arrogant and selfish, his only concern the safety of his own skin after he found he had mistakenly killed the nanny instead of his wife. It wasn't suicide that immediately came to his mind, it was simple self-preservation. Up until Veronica ran out to the Plumbers Arms he saw half a chance of getting away with it. He might have persuaded Veronica there was somebody else in the basement who had killed Sandra. His wife might have done what she said and helped him cover up the nanny's death. When Veronica ran out screaming into the street he had to think again. He could, of course, have done the honourable thing and waited for the police to arrive. He didn't. He took to his heels, not to kill himself, but to escape justice, playing for time to try and wriggle off the hook.

Last Refuge of a Scoundrel

If he did decide to kill himself he put off doing it immediately by jumping under a train or crashing his car at high speed. He made the telephone calls to his mother and Mrs Florman in Chester Square, itself a mystery because they weren't apparently made from a call box. Where did he get the money? He had left his change on the bed in his flat. Perhaps he was just fortunate and found some coins in the pocket of the old overcoat he was wearing. Most of us come across money in coats and jackets from time to time, a note tucked in the top pocket if we are lucky. Or he could have gone to see someone he knew in London and made the calls from there. We would never solve that riddle. I believe when he left No. 46 he rang Mrs Florman's doorbell and went from there to his flat in Elizabeth Street, though forensic were not able to confirm it by finding any blood stains. He had the children he had left in the house on his mind so it was logical he should make the telephone calls to Mrs Florman and his mother straight away on his own phone before rushing off. He wouldn't want any of the children going downstairs and being confronted with the blood stains in the hall and the horror in the basement. If that was the case, he didn't bother picking up anything off the bed in his flat, but we weren't to know if he grabbed any clothes or made any other hurried telephone calls.

When Lucan fled in panic from the carnage at the house in Lower Belgrave Street he had no game plan except to escape capture by the authorities and save his blood from scandal. He planned the murder of Veronica to be a success, the arrangements for the disposal of her body carefully put in place. He didn't know it would go terribly wrong and he would be on the run. When that happened everything had to be improvised, none of the players involved subsequently was chosen beforehand to play a part. He made for Uckfield and the home of the Maxwell-Scotts, either by accident in a panic or design, and spoke for some considerable time to Susan. She told the inquest on Sandra Rivett how Lucan had told her he had looked through the window and seen a man attacking his wife; he had let himself in and the man had run off. Lucan said Veronica was hysterical, crying out that someone had killed the nanny and, almost in the same breath, accusing him of having hired the man to kill her.

It was inconceivable to me that Lucan, knowing Susan Maxwell-Scott had trained as a barrister, did not question her about the legal consequences for him of the goings on in Lower

Belgrave Street he described to her. Certainly by the time he wrote the letters to Bill Shand Kydd he had calmed down sufficiently to write them in a clear way, mentioning interrupting the fight, Veronica's accusation, the circumstantial evidence against him and the fact she had demonstrated her hatred for him in the past and would do anything to see him accused. These were points that would have pleased a lawyer preparing a case in his defence if he was ever charged in court. The letters weren't written by a man in a blind panic, so emotionally disturbed he had suicide on his mind.

Lucan must have realized if the police bloodhounds caught up with him he wasn't looking at being hanged or rotting away in prison for the rest of his life. Even found guilty on a worst scenario of murdering Sandra Rivett, it is unlikely he would have received more than a ten-year jail sentence, and served only half of it. That, to my way of thinking, would not have persuaded him the only answer was to kill himself once the initial shock had worn off and he examined the situation he was in. He was at that stage evidently thinking of lesser charges of manslaughter or the attempted murder of Veronica, carrying less of a sentence even if a skilled lawyer didn't win the day and get him off altogether. In one of his letters to Bill Shand Kydd he wrote about his children seeing him standing in the dock for attempted murder. He could have completely denied the murder of Sandra and admitted the attempted murder of Veronica. There were several possibilities. The crime did not justify suicide. Why, I asked myself, would he leave Uckfield and jump in the sea when he examined the evidence against himself? If he was going to kill himself he wouldn't have even gone to Uckfield. There were nonsensical stories circulating that he got friends to kill him and dispose of his body, a ludicrous idea because I couldn't see anyone doing that and laying themselves open to a charge of murder. Nor did I think he was killed against his wishes because the people harbouring him had decided he had become too hot to handle. It was even suggested gangsters rubbed him out because of his unpaid gambling debts.

The big question I tried to answer was what Lucan did after he left Susan Maxwell-Scott. What happened in the missing hours after he left Uckfield before the car was spotted? Did he do what we were supposed to think and drive from Uckfield to Newhaven to dump Stoop's Ford Corsair? Did he go back to

London as she believed he intimated? Did he contact friends who spirited him away? I firmly believed him when he said in his letter to Bill Shand Kydd he would 'lie doggo for a bit'. I came to the conclusion he holed up somewhere and ultimately left the country, his escape engineered by a friend or friends. It wouldn't have been difficult to get out of Britain without being noticed. He wouldn't have needed to use a small boat out of a South Coast marina, a cross-channel ferry or even the *QE2*. The sort of friends Lucan had worldwide had access to large ocean-going yachts that could sail non-stop to South Africa or South America. Once there it would not be difficult for him to lose himself on vast private estates until all the fuss died down. In many remote places they would not even have heard about Lucan and, even if they had, they wouldn't be concerned about a murder in far-away London.

Top psychic Robert Cracknell, in an exclusive interview in *The Sun* in 1981, maintained Lucan was alive and well and probably living happily in Wales, protected from discovery by his VIP friends. He said: 'Although Lord Lucan initially fled abroad at the insistence of his friends, he has since returned to Britain. He is being protected by the same highly placed people who helped him escape. No way is that man dead. I don't believe for one moment that he committed suicide, he is far too stubborn and bloody-minded to have taken that way out. It wouldn't surprise me if he's walking around unrecognised in Carmarthen.' Cracknell, whose claim to fame was that he predicted the date of Yorkshire Ripper Peter Sutcliffe's last killing and the timing of his arrest, said he thought there was far more to the Lucan disappearance than met the eye and he was by no means certain Lucan did kill the nanny.

The 'third man' theory was one that refused to die down. Patrick Marnham wrote a book *Trail of Havoc* in which he said: 'There is no point in pretending that the case against Lord Lucan is not very serious. None the less, on the evidence published so far, I think it is unlikely that he murdered Sandra Rivett. In fact, in my opinion, it is quite impossible for him to have done so.' I assisted Sally Moore as she gathered material for her book *LUCAN: Not Guilty* and she was to write: 'Who killed Sandra Rivett? Twelve years after I began my own inquiry, I do not know. But I am convinced beyond reasonable doubt that Lord lucan did not murder her.' Sally Moore claimed to have spoken to a Clermont employee who saw Lucan on the steps at 9 p.m. or 9.05 at a time when he should have been at 46 Lower Belgrave Street. Naturally we were interested in interviewing the man, but we weren't able to find him despite enquiries by a team of detectives. Sally Moore was asked to name him on numerous occasions, but wouldn't say who he was. I had a feeling the mystery man was actually linkman Billy Edgson. He is the one who always came up with a time. If it was, then this version was at odds with the time of about 8.45 he had told us he spoke to Lucan.

A story about a gambling-mad baronet, deeply in debt, who vanished after a killing involving a hired killer, formed the basis of a fiction book published in 1980, *Hunted*. Veronica was upset because she thought it was based on her husband, telling the *News of the World*: 'I suppose there's nothing to stop anyone writing a novel based on Lord Lucan or any other notorious person. But at the end of the book the man is still alive, and even proud of himself. My husband isn't boasting in some foreign country where Britain doesn't have an extradition agreement.' The author, Jeremy Scott, denied he used Lucan as the model for his hero. Publication was delayed until a red wrapper could be printed to go round the book stating: '*The author and publisher wish to state that this novel is not based upon any real event and that the characters portrayed bear no relation to any persons living or dead.*'

Was there an accomplice hired by Lucan to kill Veronica, or an intruder in the house acting on his own? I could find no evidence of it. It wasn't necessary, excepting the claim by his friends he wasn't a man of violence and couldn't stand the sight of blood. I am convinced Lucan planned and carried out the operation entirely on his own, perhaps, as his friend Taki Theodoracopulos maintained, going into such fine detail as to make trial runs to determine how long Veronica's disposal would take. In domestic murders it isn't unknown for people to employ hitmen because they can't face carrying out the act themselves. If Lucan did do this I would like to know where he got the money to pay the hired killer. Patrick Marnham has suggested that is why Lucan borrowed £3,000 at an exorbitant rate of interest a few weeks before the murder. I would have thought the going rate for a hitman in 1974 would be a lot higher than that. And what has happened to the hitman since?

There was a lot of money to be made by coming forward as the 'third man', a lot more than £3,000. He could have made a fortune selling his story to the Sunday newspapers, saying: 'I was Lucan's hitman.' He would not have had to say he carried out the actual murder. Without fear of contradiction he could easily say the circumstances became such that he was there when Lucan delivered the fatal blows. At the time I dismissed the idea of a hitman mainly because it didn't explain how Lucan came to have so much blood on him.

There were some minor discrepancies in the statements over timings and the forensic evidence, but nothing I consider of major significance that can't be readily explained. It is not unusual to have some loose ends in murder inquiries where people rely on memory when they are making statements. To know the exact time people have to look at a clock or a watch and that itself has to be accurate. For Lucan an accomplice would have added a needless complication, somebody he would forever have to trust and laying himself open to the possibility of blackmail. When it comes to murder the old adage is true: if you want something doing, do it yourself. Lucan had a perfectly good blueprint worked out for murdering Veronica and disposing of her body. It is probable he would have got away with it, too, if it had gone exactly as he planned. Veronica would simply have disappeared, just like the average person who vanishes in London every week and is never found.

In 1980 BBC 2 featured Lucan as the opener of a television series called *Escape*, with actor Tony Mathews playing the earl and Janet Key appearing as Veronica. I watched it and was amused when they got Roy Ranson and myself mixed up, the actor chosen to play my part being the thin one. Writing about the programme in the *Radio Times*, Taki, who had met Lucan at the 1962 Cowes-Torquay powerboat race, said: 'I know that Lucan is dead. Lucky had often talked about the futility of living unless one lived well, or contented.' Taki, heir to a shipping fortune and a gossip columnist for *The Spectator* in the UK and the *New York Post* and *National Review* in the US, has long been regarded as one of the world's dwindling number of globe-trotting playboys and sportsmen who played Davis Cup tennis for Greece. He has a flat in Cadogan Square, Knightsbridge, and a home in New York's Manhattan and spends a third of the year in Greece, Europe and America or at sea aboard his yacht. In an interview with best-selling American writer Dominick Dunne for an article on Lucan in *Vanity Fair*, Taki said he loaned him £7,000 of his own money and raised £3,000 more from another Greek, debts that weren't included in our original financial breakdown. Taki also repeated a claim he made to Nigel Dempster in 1984, saying Lucan made two test runs to the coast carrying bags weighted to represent Veronica, transferring them from a car to a boat and dropping them out at sea.

I, too, had lunch with Dominick Dunne when he was in Britain collecting material for his article. I knew him as the man who wrote *The Two Mrs Grenvilles*, the story of a woman who shot her millionaire husband and claimed he was a prowler, which was turned into a TV series starring Claudette Colbert and Ann-Margret. Normally he spends his time circulating among the fabulously rich and famous in New York, picking up gossip for his novels which are inspired by true life crimes and expose corruption and sin among America's wealthy elite. Dunne told me how a friend of Sir James Goldsmith had quoted the billionaire businessman as saying luxury is the most addictive substance in the world. Goldsmith has his own personal paradise retreat, Cuixmala, an 18,000 acre estate carved from virgin jungle 200 miles up from Acapulco on the west coast of Mexico. The increasingly ecologically-aware financier built it after he shrewdly anticipated the stock market crash of 1987 and sold everything beforehand. Cuixmala, which friends have dubbed Xanadu, is only accessible by private plane, its barbed-wired fence patrolled by his own security staff to keep out bandits. Dunne said Goldsmith has more than 300 staff and entertains lavishly, guests able to enjoy swimming, tennis, horse riding and playing backgammon. Apart from many of the world's top businessmen, visitors to Cuixmala have included Richard Nixon and Henry Kissinger. Dunne said John Aspinall, who he regarded as Goldsmith's closest friend, is a regular guest.

Much has happened since 1974. The world has become a different place altogether. Lucan and his right-wing friends were wrong in fearing a Communist-led insurrection. The unions were to be stripped of their powers when Margaret Thatcher became Prime Minister and it was the Iron Curtain that was torn down. Lucan felt threatened by the egalitarianism of the 1970s without realizing the threat to his style of life was to come from exactly the opposite direction. The 'Thatcher Years' unleashed a new breed of entrepreneur, City whizzkids and property wheeler-dealers personified by Essex Man, who made fortunes and overwhelmed the bastions of the aristocracy by sheer weight of numbers. Yuppies, yobbo sportsmen and pop stars aped the upper classes, adopting country pursuits in rural mansions, wearing designer-label clothes, driving Rolls Royces and Porsches, buying their way into snooty clubs and jetting to once-exclusive but now crowded holiday destinations. The embattled upper class responded by going downmarket, abandoning their previous status symbols, driving battered Land Rovers and wearing scruffy clothes. Lucan, with his impeccable taste and immaculate dress sense, would have hated to see standards slip and liberal attitudes reduce everything to mediocrity.

There were still enclaves of style in the 1970s and one such place was the Marbella Club on the Costa del Sol in Spain. It was opened by Prince Alfonso von Hohenlohe Liechtenstein in the 1950s and turned the town from sleepy fishing village into a fashionable resort. I was on holiday nearby in the year after the murder and decided to pay him a visit as he knew Lucan. There were numerous private villas in the hills above Marbella where Lucan could be housed behind high walls, but I reasoned he would be unable to resist the lure of the plush casino. The Prince entertained me well but said he hadn't seen anything of Lucan.

Unfortunately the Costa del Sol was to get something of a reputation as a haven for British crooks, nicknamed the Costa del Crime with some of its property developments paid for from the proceeds of British robberies, notably the Brinks Mat bullion raid at Heathrow airport. The smart marina complex at Puerto Banûs on the outskirts of Marbella contained both the huge yachts of the mega-rich and the fast speedboats of drug smugglers crossing to and from Morocco. The coastline was poorly policed. It would have been easy for Lucan to have crossed over to Africa on a speedboat. He could equally have been aboard one of the gleaming gin-palace yachts berthed in the harbour complete with their own helicopter pads. Once Lucan had escaped from Britain the world was his oyster. Provided friends were prepared to bankroll him, Lucan held all the aces.

21 The Trial of Lord Lucan

Whoever has charge of the papers on the Lucan case at Scotland Yard will have them taken out now and again, every year or eighteen months, and have them updated. Any new information will be added and somebody will check the latest addresses of witnesses and record who has died. None of us is immortal. After twenty years several of those closely involved in the case have died. Lucan's mother, the redoubtable Dowager Countess, died in 1985, disappointed at not being able to remove the stigma of murder from her son's name. In 1978, after the Criminal Law Act of 1977 took away the right of a coroner's jury to name a murderer as a result of the Sandra Rivett inquest, the Dowager Countess unsuccessfully applied for the verdict to be set aside and another hearing held. Dr Thurston, the coroner who conducted the original inquest on Sandra Rivett, has died; so has the pathologist who performed the post-mortem and gave evidence before him, Dr Keith Simpson. Sandra's mother, Mrs Eunice Hensby, one of the last people to speak to her on the telephone, died without seeing her daughter's killer caught.

Ian Maxwell-Scott, one of Lucan's closest friends, died from a heart attack on 27 November 1993. His funeral was held at the Roman Catholic church in London's Tooting Bec. Charles Benson, now a freelance journalist who wrote a gossip column in the *Sunday Express*, suffered a mild heart attack some months later. Describing Ian Maxwell-Scott as one of the last of the great eccentrics, Benson wrote about him: 'A lifelong gambler, he lived for long shots and was never happier than when losing. He once landed a multiple bet with Ladbrokes which netted him something like £40,000 and the cheque was framed on their boardroom wall for years. Ian had experienced highs and lows of life, sadly more low than high in the past 20 years.' The Maxwell-Scotts long ago sold Grants Hill House at Uckfield and sheltered old people's bungalows have now been built on the land.

It may be Lucan himself is now dead, either as a result of an accident or through natural causes. On 18 December 1994 he would celebrate his sixtieth birthday, but he might have succumbed to an unhealthy lifestyle of drinking and smoking. His wife, Veronica, now lives in the mews house at Eaton Row while 46 Lower Belgrave Street was sold and has new occupants. In 1982 custody of her two younger children was transferred to the Shand Kydds. Veronica is now seldom seen by her neighbours. More happily, the three children have done well, brought up as wards of court under the guidance of the Shand Kydds, as Lucan requested in his letter, with financial contributions from friends. Lady Frances went to Bristol University and is now a solicitor specializing in corporate law, Lord Bingham went to Trinity, Cambridge, after Eton to read English and works for merchant banker's Kleinwort Benson, and Lady Camilla has read classics at Balliol College, Oxford, to complete her education. Seven years after Lucan disappeared an application could have been made for him to be declared dead and Lord Bingham would have inherited the earldom. An application was not made until 1994, but moves were going on at that time in the High Court to have Lord Lucan legally 'sworn to be dead' so family solicitors could at last sort out his complex estate, said to be worth £2 million to £3 million on paper. Rents on the dilapidated cottages and houses on the Castlebar estate in County Mayo continue not to be paid and, while individually small, run up to hundreds of thousands of pounds because there are so many of them. The tenants refuse to pay anyone but their absentee landlord Lucan, local county councillor Dick Morrin saying in 1991: 'The easy money we gave him got him into bad habits like gambling. If we had cut off his source earlier he might not have ended up the way he did.'

Sir James Goldsmith finally achieved his ambition to get into politics, not in Britain, but in France where he was elected a Member of the European Parliament in June, 1994. The crusading multi-millionaire accepted an invitation to join Phillippe de Villiers, a right-wing member of the French Assembly, and Charles de Gaulle, grandson of the famous General, to fight in the European Elections with the new L'Autre Europe party. They fought an anti-Maastricht campaign, determined to strip away the powers of the European

Union and halt what they see as a march towards a federal Europe. In the election L'Autre Europe surprised political pundits by doing remarkably well, picking up 12.3 per cent of the French vote and 13 seats at Strasbourg. A glittering celebrity-packed party attended by Princess Diana was held at the Ritz to celebrate Goldsmith's election as a Euro MP and Annabel's sixtieth birthday.

Mark Birley, whose wife Annabel became the mistress and then the wife of Goldsmith after their divorce in 1975, has continued to be a leading light on the London social scene. Annabel's celebrated its thirtieth anniversary in 1993, still laying claim to being the world's most exclusive disco. Occasionally it gets into the headlines, like the time in 1986 when Princess Diana and Sarah Ferguson turned up dressed as women police officers just before 'Fergie' married Prince Andrew. Birley has built up his empire, adding a new restaurant, Harry's Bar, to Annabel's and Mark's Club and branching out into sport with the opening of the Bath and Racquets Club in Mayfair in 1989.

John Aspinall returned to the gambling scene, opening the Aspinall Curzon Club in what had been the home of his present wife, Lady Sarah Curzon. He remained loyal to his old friends from the Clermont days, Ian Maxwell-Scott managing the wine cellar and Daniel Meinertzhagen the restaurant and non-gambling activities. In a niche in one of the dining rooms they erected a bust of Lucan with a plaque of Aspinall's oft-quoted TV conversation with Ludovic Kennedy about Lucan: 'What would you do if he walked into the room? ... I would embrace him.' Aspinall sold the club in 1987 before the stock market crash, but retained a seat on the board. He used his share of the money, reportedly £35 million, to help finance the £4,000-a-day running costs of his zoos. His mother, the colourful Lady O, died in 1987. Meinertzhagen's family suffered a personal tragedy in 1992 when his 16-year-old daughter, Georgina, fell to her death from the window of her student lodgings at Oxford after drinking 17 glasses of tequila in a wine bar at a birthday party. Among Lucan's other friends, Susan Maxwell-Scott lives in London, Greville Howard at King's Lynn, Norfolk, and Selim Zilka in California. Andrina Colquhoun worked for the designer Terence Conran for a time before becoming the personal assistant of best-selling author Jeffrey Archer. Lucan's brother, Hugh, went out to South Africa, where he lives in Johannesburg and works for the government.

All of the principal police officers on the Lucan Murder Squad have retired from the force and are now engaged on other activities. Roy Ranson left to work for the BBC as their security adviser at Portland Place before retiring again. Graham Forsyth works as an insurance investigator for a firm of loss adjusters and his work takes him abroad. John Hefford had a firm of private investigators before his death in 1994 and Sally Bower retired from the police in 1994. I retired and ran the George and Dragon public house at Chipstead in Kent with my wife from 1980 to 1990, still keeping active as secretary of the Sevenoaks Licensed Victuallers Association.

Over the years Lucan's name has continued to get into the newspapers. In 1988 a letter purporting to have been written by society transvestite Vikki de Lambray to the Dowager Countess got into the hands of the *Sunday Mirror*. De Lambray died from an overdose of sleeping pills two years earlier and, with an open verdict at the inquest, the paper said friends believed he was murdered. In the letter de Lambray said he was with Lucan when the earl died in North Wales in August, 1979. Lucan had written a number of letters and these, together with photographs and a tape recording made three hours before his death, he asked to be released to the *Press Association* exactly ten years later in 1989. De Lambray said the evidence was in a safe-deposit box in a bank in the north of England, but the police were never able to find it or any link between him and Lucan. De Lambray said Lucan told him who actually did kill Sandra Rivett but, as he wrote the letter while in prison awaiting trial for cheque frauds and was an outrageous con man, it was hard to believe anything he said. Six years earlier, in 1982, John Miller, the man who abducted Great Train Robber Ronald Biggs in Brazil, claimed he was holding Lucan in the Caribbean. This turned out to be a hoax, his 'Lucan' an actor with a stuck-on moustache. Until he is located, new stories will continue to be told about Lucan and he will go on being sighted all over the world. In 1993 John Sinclair, Viscount Thurson's heir, said in the *Daily Mail Diary* so many people were mistaking him for Lucan at the country house hotel he runs in Sussex that his wife was thinking of getting him a T-shirt saying: I AM NOT LORD LUCAN.

* * *

People say everything is relative, so when Lucan wrote in his letter he would 'lie doggo for a bit', he could have meant two days or twenty years. Having been away for the equivalent of two of what people popularly know as 'life sentences' of ten years, he may now be minded to return and give himself up to the authorities. Any lawyer worth his salt would advise against it, saying: 'If you are enjoying life, stay where you are.' Lucan wasn't the sort of exile who would miss his pie and mash on the Old Kent Road. The dissolute lifestyle he enjoyed is available in many parts of the world. But it is conceivable he may wish to return to clear his family name of the slur of murder. It is even possible he will be apprehended somewhere, though this is less probable with the passing years as he is now likely to be unrecognizable – portly, heavily-jowled and almost bald. He has eluded the law this long, he can doubtless continue to do so for the rest of his days. His friends, and he had many all over the world, got the better of us. At the end of the day, they won and we lost. I don't believe we ever came anywhere near to capturing him. It should rankle with me, but it doesn't. I don't worry about things like that. I was doing a professional job and you soon learn as a detective you are not going to win every time. It was my job to catch wrongdoers, but there were many times I saw people I knew to be guilty walk free from court. When juries go out to deliberate, most members have no idea whether the person in the dock is guilty or not guilty and what their verdict will be. But I would still like to see Lucan put on trial and convicted to avenge the death of Sandra Rivett. She was a young woman who died in the prime of her life for no other reason than Lucan's gambling debts and his hatred for his wife.

If Lucan was to return to Britain, either by arrangement on his own initiative or reluctantly picked up and extradited, what would happen to him today? For a start he would immediately be arrested as he stepped off the plane to a glare of camera flashlights because the warrants for his arrest are still on file. He would appear at the Old Bailey where he was committed from the inquest. Whether or not bail would be considered would depend on the circumstances of his arrest, if he voluntarily gave himself up or was captured. Without bail Lucan would have a problem, facing months on remand in prison because it would be a long time before the case came before the Central Criminal Court. As he sat twiddling his thumbs in prison, a

Balaclava-sized legal battle would rage on how he could be given a fair trial. There is no way it could happen. Carts and horses have been driven through the laws of *sub judice* through scores of books, TV programmes and newspaper articles. Where could an unprejudiced jury be found to try the case?

With that hurdle eventually overcome, the Director of Public Prosecutions would be faced with a major problem over the evidence to be presented at the trial. Some of the witnesses have died. The defence would be unable to challenge their evidence and could object to their statements being admitted. Those who are still alive would have to be seen and asked to make a new statement saying if they wished to alter, add to or correct their original statements. There are dozens of witnesses who would have to be seen. After more than twenty years they could easily say they did not recall making a statement in the first place, let alone what they said in it. If this happened, in court, on the witnesses stand, they would be confronted by the prosecution with their original statement, asked to confirm it was their signature on it and requested to read the contents out to the jury. If they didn't deny making the statement altogether, they could say they had absolutely no memory of what they said at the time and so would be unable to answer questions. At the inquest, only seven months after the murder, Lucan's mother, the Dowager Countess, had difficulty in remembering details of her conversation with Sergeant Forsyth on the night in question.

Given the change in the law over an inquest jury naming a murderer, it might be a decision would be taken that the interests of justice would be better served by having Lucan recommitted for trial from a magistrate's court. Magistrates would test the evidence to see if a trial was justified. The whole situation would be unprecedented, a legal minefield. At the inquest there were times when the jury was sent out while the barristers debated points of law. If Lucan came to court the lawyers would have a field day; the arguments could go on and on and the jury would be in and out like yo-yos. The basic law remains that Veronica could give evidence against Lucan for assaulting her, but not for murdering Sandra. Veronica's entire story has been told so many times everyone knows about it. The trial would be a farce, a huge waste of public money. If Lucan was found guilty the penalty would depend to some extent on what he has been doing for the past twenty years, whether or not he has been living a life of luxury. If he said he had suffered terrible nightmares, waking up in a cold sweat every night tortured by what he had done, he would get sympathy and might get off with a token sentence. At worst, given the more liberal outlook on sentencing today than in the 1970s, Lucan would likely get no more than a maximum five years jail sentence, serving just two-and-a-half years behind bars.

I have been to the Old Bailey many times so it is not hard for me to visualize the oak-panelled No. 1 Court that many famous murderers have been taken from and subsequently hanged. In my mind's eye I can see Lucan standing in the dock looking down over the brass rail at the courtroom, its leather seats crowded to capacity. As I imagine him, he looks considerably different than in his original photographs, but has grown his moustache back while awaiting trial. It is the end of what has been a sensational case going on for months, Lucan pleading Not Guilty and every detail reported avidly by the media now eagerly awaiting the result. As I had expected, Lucan had been represented by a heavyweight counsel who was a household name with a reputation for seldom losing a case. He hadn't missed a trick in his cross-examination of our prosecution witnesses. Veronica had been on the witness stand for three days, closely questioned about her psychiatric treatment and her relationship with her husband. Lucan did not have to give evidence, but much play was made of the fact he chose to do so on oath. He came across as an imposing figure as he was skilfully led by questions from his barrister in relentless pursuit of his 'third man' defence. My evidence was used not to repudiate the story, but twisted round to support it. Similarly, the technical evidence of the forensic witnesses about the blood in the basement was turned to Lucan's advantage. Not surprisingly, when Lucan's friends were on the stand facing cross-examination by prosecuting counsel, they seemed to have been smitten by an epidemic of amnesia so severe I was amazed they could remember their names.

In his long and eloquent final address Lucan's counsel summed up some of the salient points in his defence:

> Members of the jury, you have heard from Lady Lucan how, after the break-up of their marriage, she would sometimes see

her husband driving past the house wearing dark glasses. In his evidence to you, Lord Lucan freely admits this, saying he was concerned for the safety of his children. He further says on the night of the unfortunate death of Sandra Rivett he walked past the house and, seeing what looked like a torch shining in the basement, decided to investigate. As a result he saw what he took to be a fight going on.

Counsel pauses, looks in my direction and continues:

Much play has been made by the prosecution, based on evidence of ex-Detective Chief Inspector David Gerring, that it was not possible to see a struggle going on in the basement through the slats in the venetian blinds in the window. I strongly refute that. Sufficient could be seen for Lord Lucan to see something unusual was happening. By kneeling down he could clearly see a scuffle taking place in the torchlight. Support for this comes from forensic evidence that shows the exact spot where he said it was occurring was where directional blood splashes on the walls point to Sandra Rivett being attacked. On seeing what he thought to be Lady Lucan being assaulted, Lord Lucan has described to you how he let himself in through the front door and went down the stairs to the basement. On reaching the bottom of the stairs he saw a man by then stuffing a body into a canvas bag. He went to grab the man, but slipped on what must have been the blood on the floor. The man rushed past him and ran up the stairs, hitting him a heavy blow in the stomach with the torch and knocking him to the blood-stained floor. Winded and in considerable pain, he could hear Lady Lucan shouting out at the top of the stairs, presumably the same cries which Lady Frances heard from her bedroom. When Lord Lucan had recovered sufficiently to go up the stairs to the hall it was to find Lady Lucan in a bemused and hysterical state accusing him of attacking her. Lord Lucan tried to calm her down by putting his arms round her, getting further blood on his clothes in the process, and they went up together to her bedroom.

What happened immediately after that is not in dispute, Lady Lucan ran from the house and Lord Lucan left the scene. He said in a letter to Bill Shand Kydd, written that night, that he felt the circumstantial evidence against him was strong and his wife would say it was all his doing. He said Lady Lucan had demonstrated her hatred for him in the past and would do anything to see him accused. Lord Lucan is still strongly of that view today, he has repeated that assertion to you under oath in the witness box. When Lady Lucan gave her evidence I took the opportunity to question her closely about their troubled relationship that led to their separation. You have heard in some detail of her long history of psychiatric treatment, both before and since this incident. I suggest when she was attacked, in darkness, by this unknown intruder she was rendered briefly unconscious by blows to the head, similar blows to those that killed Sandra Rivett. The man then escaped by leaving through the front door. Lady Lucan came round to find her husband at her side so wrongly, but perfectly understandably in her dazed state, assumed he was her assailant. She then became convinced of it against the weight of evidence only because of her consuming hatred of her husband.

After a further pause he goes on:

Many years have passed since these events and memories have dimmed. Some of the people who made statements to the police at that time are, unhappily, no longer with us; they have passed on. We have been denied the benefit of hearing what they have to say and to question them, but Lord Lucan insisted that their original statements be read to you. The witnesses you have seen are all that much older than they were in 1974 and 1975, so it is understandable their recollection of what they did or did not say in statements to the police all that time ago is, at best, hazy. In some cases their memory has deserted them altogether. I am sure some of you on the jury have elderly relatives and are aware how, sadly, this does happen in later life as faculties fail.

Lord Lucan, a man of hitherto unblemished character from one of our oldest and most respected families, stands before you an innocent man. He is a victim of mistaken identity who has himself suffered significant distress over many years because of a fear he would be wrongfully detained and our much-vaunted system of British justice would fail him.

At the end of the summing up the jury would retire for a long time to consider their verdict. There are two schools of thought on what this means, some saying there is more chance of a conviction, others that members are arguing among themselves and can't make up their minds. In court the atmosphere is electric. Outside the courthouse banks of cameras are lined up and reporters wait tensely to conduct their interviews. Finally the all-male jury files back into their seats and their foreman remains standing. The Clerk of the Court looks across at him and asks solemnly: 'Have you reached a verdict?'

'Yes,' says the foreman. 'Not guilty.'

Index

Ann-Margret, 178
Anne, Her Royal Highness The Princess Royal, 20
Archer, Jeffrey, 182
Aspinall, John (Aspers), 41, 42, 73, 97–8, 109, 119, 148, 178; Clermont Club, 71–2, 79–81; meeting of *Five Just Men*; loyalty to Lucan, 140–2; eulogy for Dominic Elwes, 168–9
Aspinall, Col. Robert, 140
Autogyro x-ray search, 143

Baddick, PC Christopher, 13, 25, 36
Bad Neuenahr, 39
Baker, Sgt. Donald, 13
Ball, Ian, 20
Barley Mow public house, 152, 158
Barraclough, Kenneth, 118
Belgravia, 19, 23, 29, 66, 68, 133
Benson, Charles, 73, 100, 115, 148, 180
Beowulf, 169
Betting and Gaming Act, 42, 71
Biggs, Ronnie, 102, 183
Bingham, Lady Camilla, 13, 18, 36, 48, 51–2, 58, 62, 63–4, 67, 76–8, 81–2, 85, 86, 124, 181
Bingham, Charles, 32
Bingham, Lady Frances, 13, 18, 36, 43, 44, 47, 48, 50, 57–8, 62, 63–4, 67, 76–8, 81–2, 85, 86, 124, 181, 187; statement, 50–2
Bingham, Lord George, 13, 18, 36, 48, 51–2, 62, 63–4, 67, 76–8, 81–2, 85, 86, 98, 124, 181
Bingham, George Charles Patrick (Pat), 6th Earl of Lucan, 38, 55
Bingham, Hugh, 73, 77, 183
Bingham, Capt. John, 32
Bingham, Sir Richard, 32
Bingham, Robert de, 31
Birkett, Peter, 102, 104
Birley, Lady Annabel (Later Lady Annabel Goldsmith), 79, 142, 148–50, 182
Birley, Mark, 73, 79, 150, 166, 182
Birley, Robin, 142
Blanco, Admiral Luis Careero, 89
Bond, James, 56, 143
Bostock, Sgt. John, 93
Bower, Woman DC Sally, 50, 81, 111, 183

Boyce, Nicholas, 82
Brandt, William, 40, 41, 42
Brandt, Willy, 89
Broccoli, Cubby, 56
Bruce, Maj.-Gen. George McIlree, 141
Burden, Peter, 102
Burke's Peerage, 18
Byron, Lord, 153

Cadogan, Lord, 18
Caine, Michael, 56
MV *Captain de Gough*, 102
Cardigan, Lord, 33–4
Caremoli, Brigitte, 161–2
Castlebar, County Mayo, 32, 33, 34, 122, 181
Chapman, Stanley, 13
Charles, His Royal Highness The Prince of Wales, 31
Chelsea set, 41
Cherbourg, 159–63
Chilton Nursery Training College, 56
Clark, Sir Andrew, 120
Clermont Club, 42, 71–2, 79–81, 83–7, 88, 91, 97, 119, 128, 131–2, 141, 148–9, 163, 182
Cluff, Algy, 110
Colbert, Claudette, 178
Coles, Bruce, 153–7
Colquhoun, Andrina (Andy), 73, 82, 182
Comfort, Jimmy, *see* Cumerford, Jimmy, 118
Compton, Lord, 164–5
Connery, Sean, 56
Conran, Terence, 182
Coolican, Don, 165
Cornell, George, 27
Courage, Piers, 164
Coward, Noel, 19
Cracknell, Robert, 175
Crockett, Davy, 13
Cubitt, Thomas, 68
Cuixmala, Mexico, 178
Cumerford, Jimmy, *see* Comfort, Jimmy, 118
Curzon, Lady Charlotte, 164
Curzon, Lady Sarah (Sally), 164, 182

Dawson, Edward, 50
Deauville, 41
Debrett's Peerage, 18
Deen, John, 164
Deen, Rupert, 164
de Lambray, Vikki, 183

Index

Delfont, Sir Bernard, 127
DeLima, DS David, 59
Demetriou, Andrew, 83–4
Dempster, Harry, 136
Dempster, Nigel, 164, 178
de Sica, Vittorio, 56
de Villiers, Phillippe, 181
Diana, Her Royal Highness The Princess of Wales, 31, 182
Dieppe, 60, 96, 102–5
Duke of Wellington public house (Duke of Boots), 66, 101, 136, 152
Duncan, Maj. Charles Moorehouse, 54
Duncan, Thelma, *see* Margrie, Thelma, 54
Dunne, Dominick, 178

Eastham, Michael, 153–7
Edgar, David, 11
Edgson, William (Billy), 83–4, 86, 176
El Morocco Club, New York, 148
Elwes, Dominic, 68, 73, 79, 115–16, 131, 169; elopement, 41, 131, 133; ostracized, 147–50; plea to Lucan, 163–5; suicide, 166–7; memorial service, 167–9

Falcon, Joe, *see* Fitzpatrick, Michael, 117–19
Famine in Ireland, 33–4
Ferguson, Sarah (later The Duchess of York), 182
Fielder, Mike, 102
Fitzpatrick, Michael, *see* Joe Falcon, 117–19
Florman, Madelaine, 68, 173
Ford, President Gerald, 12, 125
Forsyth, DS Graham, 17–18, 20, 26, 28–9, 35–7, 43, 50, 77, 81, 118, 152, 183, 185
Fox, James, 73, 101, 147–50, 152, 163, 164, 170
Fürstenberg, Gustav and Paula von, 148

Gardner, Jennifer, 25
Gardner, Margery, 27
Gaskell, Tom Milnes, 99
George and Dragon public house, 183
Gerald Road police station, 13, 17, 18, 26, 46, 117
Gibbs, Lady Sarah, 78, 117–18, 152
Gibbs, the Revd William, 78, 158–9
Gilbert, Cdr. Vic, 132
Gilson, Dennis, 139

Giscard d'Estaing, Valery, 89
Gladstone Smith, Peter, 117
Goldsmith, Jimmy (later Sir James), 41, 73, 97–8, 127–8, 164, 166, 178, 181–2; Acapulco house party, 79, 148–50; election to European Parliament, 181–2; knighthood, 127–8; *Private Eye* libel action, 128
Goldsmith, Teddy, 98, 127
Gomez, Gen. Francesco da Costa, 89
Grade, Lew, 127
Grants Hill House, Uckfield, 52, 111, 112
Greenstreet, Sydney, 160
Gregson, Michael, 27
Guilpain, Suzanne, 161

Haigh, John, 27
Hanratty, James, 27
Hanson, Jimmy, 166
Hawser, Lewis, 171
Heath, Neville, 27
Heath, Ted (later Sir Edward), 12, 88–9
Hefford, DS John, 20, 46, 134, 183
Hefner, Hugh, 71–2
Hensby, Albert, 152–3
Hensby, Eunice, 56–7, 124, 159, 180
Hicks Beach, Michael, 73, 83–4
Hill, Dr Brian, 144–6
Hill, Caroline, 74, 76
Hill, Graham, 167
Hitler, Adolf, 88, 90
Hohenlohe, Prince Alfonso von, 179
Holy Trinity Church, Brompton, 54
Hood, Robin, 15
House, Chris, 102
Howard, Greville, 26, 74, 85–7, 105, 139, 151, 155–6, 170, 182
Howe, Lord, 164
Hulls, DI Charlie, 58, 59

Ingrams, Richard, 169–71
Interpol, 30, 159–60

Jackson, Glenda, 134
Jackson, Marguerite, 58
Jenkins, Roy, 100

Kagan, Joseph, 127
Kennedy, President John, 17
Kennedy, Tessa, 41, 133
Kent, William, 80
Key, Janet, 177

Index

King's Arms public house, 11
Kissinger, Henry, 178
Knight, John, 161
Knight, Kenneth, 134
Kotlarova, Jordanka, 64
Kray, Ronnie, 27
Krefeld, Germany, 38

Laleham Golf Club, 122
Lazenby, George, 56
Le Touquet, 41
Leverton, David, 65
Lord's View, St John's Wood, 25
Lucan, 3rd Earl of, 32–5, 122, 172
Lucan, 6th Earl of (George Charles Patrick/Pat), 31, 38, 40, 42–3, 55
Lucan, the Dowager Countess of (Kaitilin/Kait), 18–19, 47, 49–50, 75, 112, 152, 173, 180, 185; telephone calls from Lucan, 25–6, 35–7, 173; marriage and politics, 42–3
Lucan, the Countess of (Veronica/V), 17, 22–4, 35–6, 47, 48, 50–2, 56–8, 72, 75–6, 79, 87, 97–9, 101, 106, 115, 121, 124, 139, 142, 172–4, 181, 186–8; birth of children, 62; breaks her silence, 136–8; collapse in Plumbers Arms, 12–14, 29–30, 155–6; Clermont Widow's Table, 62–3; escape to the country, 81–2; details of the attack on her, 13–14, 44–5, 58–9, 112, 136, 155–6, 172, 185; dispute over children, 63–4, 76–8; hospital treatment, 24–5, 28–9; at Sandra Rivett's inquest, 135, 150–9; marriage to Lucan, 54–6; marriage breakdown, 63–4; first meeting with Lucan, 55; mental state, 63, 70, 83, 85–6, 115, 137–8, 147, 158, 181, 186–8; split with Lucan, 79; statement to police, 43–5
Lipton, Marcus, 100
Liston, Sonny, 55
Llewellyn, Dai, 71
Llewellyn, Sir Harry 'Foxhunter', 71
Lownes, Victor, 72
Lumley, Joanna, 79

Maclaine, Shirley, 56
Makarious, Archbishop, 89
Marbella, 179
Margaret, Her Royal Highness Princess, 41
Margrie, James, 54

Margrie, Thelma, *see* Duncan, Thelma, 54
Marina, Princess, 41
Marnham, Patrick, 170–1, 175–7
Martin, Christabel (later Mrs Christabel Boyce), 81
Masters, Brian, 140
Mathews, Tony, 177
Maxwell-Scott, Ian, 48, 52, 69, 74, 111–14, 119–21, 129, 180; interview at Gerald Road, 119–20
Maxwell-Scott, Susan, 48, 52–3, 60, 69, 74, 91, 95, 97–8, 107, 119–21, 138, 154, 173–4, 182; gives Lucan sleeping pills, 120–1; hoax telegram, 138; interview at Grants Hill House, 110–14
Meinertzhagen, Daniel, 74, 115, 164, 182
Mercer, Agnes, 66
Mercer, Joe, 66
Mercer, John, 66
Miller, Eric, 126–7
Miller, John, 183
Mitchum, Robert, 80
Moore, Sally, 175–6
Morgan, DC Robert, 20, 27–8, 59
Morrin, Dick, 181
Muhammad Ali (Cassius Clay), 55

Neil, DC Alec, 59
Newhaven, 48, 59–61, 65, 92–6, 102–3, 105, 107, 133, 143, 174
Nixon, President Richard, 12, 125, 178
Nob Squad, 128–30
Norland College, 56

O'Donnell, Mary-Geraldine (Mary-O), 77, 98
Olausen, Cevald, 13
Orient Express, 55
Osborne, Lady (Lady O), 80, 109, 140

Patino, Isabel, 41
Penrose, John, 101, 144
Penwood, Westchester, 40
Pereira, Dr Margaret, 75–6
Peron, President Juan, 89
Phillips, Anthony, 99
Phillips, Capt. Mark, 20
Pittaway, DCS Stan, 160
Playboy, 71–2, 119
Plumber's Arms public house, 11–14, 29–30, 57, 155, 172
Police Five, 9

Pompidou, Georges, 89
Powell, Enoch, 85
Powell-Brett, Dr Christopher, 25
Price, DI Cyril, 93

QE2, 163, 175

Raglan, Lord, 32, 110
Ranson, DCS Roy, 18–21, 27, 46–9, 58–9, 64–5, 74, 92, 96, 110–11, 123, 125–6, 138, 159, 162, 172, 177, 183
Raphael, Stephen, 74, 115, 148
Rayne, Sir Max, 127
Read, Frank, 66
Red Alert, 30
Rees, Mr Justice, 77
Rhys-Evans, Glynne, 160, 162
Rivett, Roger, 28, 57
Rivett, Sandra, 17, 29, 35, 44–5, 46, 47, 50–2, 56–60, 68, 75–6, 82, 85–7, 117, 126, 129, 136, 137, 139, 167, 170, 172, 174, 175, 183, 184, 185, 187; background, 56–7; funeral service, 123–5; inquest, 134–6, 150–7, 159, 180; post-mortem, 27–8; relationship with Lady Lucan, 90–1
Rodd, Tremayne, 169
Rogers, Reggie, 160, 163
Rossiter, Leonard, 107
Royal Artillery barracks, 11
Russell, Evelyn, 65, 74

St George's Hospital, 13, 17, 24, 28, 76, 115, 119
St Malo, 162
St Swithin's School, Winchester, 54
Sawicka, Stefanja, 64
Schmidt, Helmut, 89
Scott, Sir Walter, 120
Selassie, Haile, 89
Sellers Peter, 56
Shand Kydd, Bill, 35, 40, 47–9, 55, 65, 70, 74, 99, 112–13, 115–16, 152, 154–5, 174–5, 187
Shand Kydd, Christina, 48, 54–5, 74, 77, 99, 152, 154
Simpson, Professor Keith, 27–8, 180
Sirica, Judge, 12
Smith, Dr Michael, 24
Soames, Nicholas, 148
Stirling, Col. David, 89, 131–2

Stonehouse, John, 106, 133–4
Stoop, Michael, 37, 49, 66–8, 74
Storie, Valerie, 27
Strahan, Frederick, 13
Summers, Owen, 101, 136, 144, 163
Sutcliffe, Peter, 175

Thatcher, Margaret (later Lady Thatcher), 178–9
Theodoracopulos, Taki, 176–8
Thomas, William, 155, 157
Thorne, Frank, 165
Thurston, Dr Gavin, 134–5, 150–8, 167, 180
Tillyer, Father Desmond, 77
Traini, Bob, 101
Tucker, Margaret Brady (Aunt Marcia), 39–40, 73
Tullet, Tom, 101
Turner, Norman, 77
Tynan, Kenneth, 167–8

Ustinov, Peter, 168

MV *Valencay*, 103
Ventura, Viviane, 71
MV *Viking 1*, 160
Villa Palladium, 163, 165, 166
Vine, Brian, 100–1, 135–6

Wallace, Edgar, 115
Ward, Vera, 152–3
Warner, Jack, 19
Watergate, 12, 125
Watling, Brian, 153, 156
Webster, David, 153
West, Peter, 148
Westminster, Duke of, 18
Wheatsheaf Hotel, 54
Whitehouse, Derrick, 12, 29–30
White Migrant, 40
Who's Who, 18, 31
Wilde, Oscar, 169
Williams, Marcia (later Lady Falkender), 126–8
Wilson, Harold, 12, 88, 125–8, 144, 171
Withers, Sgt. Ron, 93
Woodham-Smith, Cecil, 43
Wright, George, 164
Wyndham, Melissa, 167